Property

The idea of property carries both extensive symbolic resonance and significant practical implications in contemporary Western societies. Legal works on property emphasise formal legal regimes of property ownership, while philosophical treatments focus upon moral and economic justifications for property. *Property: Meanings, Histories, Theories* examines property in a cultural, symbolic and historical framework. One aim of the book is to outline the ways in which concepts of property are symbolically and practically connected to social relations of power. A second aim is to consider and critique the 'objects' of property in changing material contexts. Third, the book explores challenges to the Western idea of property posed by colonial and post-colonial contexts, such as the disempowerment through property of whole cultures, the justifications for colonial expansion, and biopiracy. These themes are considered in three central chapters dealing with the meanings of property, its history, and philosophical accounts of property. A final chapter considers some alternative narratives of property and possibilities for its reconstruction.

Margaret Davies is Professor of Law at Flinders University, South Australia. Her research covers several fields of legal theory, including feminist legal theory, legal pluralism, the philosophy of property, and postmodernism. She is the author of several books, including *Asking the Law Question* (2002) and *Delimiting the Law* (1996).

Property

Meanings, histories, theories

Margaret Davies

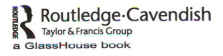
Routledge·Cavendish
Taylor & Francis Group
a GlassHouse book

First published 2007
by Routledge-Cavendish
2 Park Square, Milton Park, Abingdon, Oxon OX14 4RN

Simultaneously published in the USA and Canada
by Routledge-Cavendish
270 Madison Ave, New York, NY 10016

*Routledge-Cavendish is an imprint of the Taylor & Francis Group,
an informa business*

© 2007 Davies, Margaret

A GlassHouse book

Typeset in Times by
RefineCatch Limited, Bungay, Suffolk
Printed and bound in Great Britain by
TJ International Ltd, Padstow, Cornwall

British Library Cataloguing in Publication Data
A catalogue record for this book is available from the British Library

Library of Congress Cataloging in Publication Data
Davies, Margaret (Margaret Jane)
   Property : meanings, histories, theories / Margaret Davies.
     p. cm.
   Includes bibliographical references and index.
   ISBN-13: 978-1-904-385-84-4 (pbk. : alk. paper)
   ISBN-10: 1-904385-84-2 (pbk. : alk. paper)
   ISBN-13: 978-0-415-42933-7 (hardback : alk. paper)
   ISBN-10: 0-415-42933-1 (hardback : alk. paper)
   [etc.]
1. Property.   I. Title.

   K720.D38 2008
   346.04-dc22

                        2007024475

ISBN10: 1-904385-84-2 (pbk)
ISBN13: 978-1-904385-84-4 (pbk)

ISBN10: 0-415-42933-1 (hbk)
ISBN13: 978-0-415-42933-7 (hbk)

eISBN10: 0-203-93731-7
eISBN13: 978-0-203-93731-0

Contents

Acknowledgements

I have received invaluable assistance from a number of people. I would like to thank David Bamford, Tina Dolgopol, Gary Davis, Natalie Fowell, Mary Heath, Eric Richards, Kathy Mack, Ngaire Naffine and Andrew Stewart for providing some useful references and resources, and indulging in conversations about different aspects of this book. I would also like to thank Judith Bannister for reading and providing feedback on the intellectual property material in Chapter 3. Excellent research assistance has been provided by Reetvinder Randhawa, Debbie Bletsas, and Christina Son. At Routledge-Cavendish, Colin Perrin has been most encouraging. And Liz Rawlings has as always been extremely patient and supportive.

In particular, I would like to thank Davina Cooper, Jane Knowler and Lesley Petrie for reading the entire draft at very short notice and under a limited timeframe, and for providing many useful comments, criticisms, and suggestions.

The author and publisher are grateful for permission to reproduce short excerpts from the following articles:

Davies, M., 'Queer Property, Queer Persons: Self-Ownership and Beyond' (1999) 8 *Social and Legal Studies* 327–52

Davies, M., 'The Proper: Discourses of Purity' (1998) 9 *Law and Critique* 147–73

Davies, M. 'The Common Law Culture of Property and Propriety', *Rättsculturer – rapport från ett seminarium: Skrifter från Juridiska institutionen vid Umeå universitet* No 5/2001, 33–43.

Chapter 1

Critiques

INTRODUCTION

I can't help it, I am going to begin the book with a cliché, nothing less than the most obvious starting point for a book on property and the most over-quoted piece of prose on the topic, by William Blackstone:

> There is nothing which so generally strikes the imagination, and engages the affections of mankind as the right of property; or that sole and despotic dominion which one man claims and exercises over the external things of the world, in total exclusion of the right of any other individual in the universe. And yet there are very few, that will give themselves the trouble to consider the original and foundation of this right. Pleased as we may be with the possession, we seem afraid to look back to the means by which it was acquired, as if fearful of some defect in our title; or at best we rest satisfied with the decision of the laws in our favour, without examining the reason or authority upon which those laws have been built.
>
> (Blackstone 1766: 2)

There are a number of good reasons for this being such a well-known quotation. It raises, in a very succinct form, quite a few of the issues which many discussions of property raise. For instance: are 'we' (meaning in this context the Western liberal 'we') really as obsessed with property as Blackstone claims? If so, why? In what sense is it a 'sole and despotic dominion'? Can only 'external things' be property, or can we own ourselves? Is it really about such 'total exclusion' of everyone? Why are we so wilfully blind to the justifications for property and so dogmatic about the rights associated with it? Do we really have a deep-seated fear that we do not in fact have a very good moral or other right to whatever it is we think we own? When distributions of property are so manifestly unequal, we do not need to go very far to find a source for such a fear: although politicians, philosophers, ideologues and others may find it equally easy to dream up justifications, a persistent doubt about entitlement remains.

The following somewhat different description of property emphasises obligations towards others, rather than rights exercised 'in total exclusion' of them:

> The ability to control one's property can promote human dignity, individual fulfillment, and social welfare. Yet the various tensions embedded in the property system require us to impose obligations on owners – obligations to use their property in a manner that is not inimical to the legitimate interests of others. Entitlement initially appears to abhor obligation, yet on reflection we can see that it requires it. Indeed, it is the tension between ownership and obligation that is the essence of property.
>
> (Singer 2000: 204)

This more modern understanding of property insists upon its relational dimension. Property is not just about individuals exercising control over external things and (therefore) over others. Rather, property concerns individuals *and* communities: how they are formed, how they live together, and how they use their resources. On this understanding, property brings into play an entire social order.

This book will consider a range of issues raised by these, and other, interpretations of property. In doing so, it takes as its focal point property *theory*, rather than property *law*. Of course, to the extent that Anglocentric[1] property theory is based upon a culturally distinctive common law approach to property, occasional reference to property law will be useful and necessary. But, as I hope to show in the following chapters, the concept and the manifestations of property in the Western liberal context go far beyond legal doctrine, extending to ideologies of the self, social interactions with others, concepts of law, and social concepts of gender roles and race relations. More generally, as Carol Rose has shown, cultural narratives about ourselves and our environment play an important role in influencing or persuading the community about different notions of property (1994: 1–7). While this short book aims centrally to provide an overview of critical approaches to property, it also proposes a particular approach to understanding property as a cultural as well as a legal phenomenon. Put simply, that approach is pluralistic in that it rejects the idea that there can be a single explanation or theory of property. Rather, I will present property as a multi-faceted, sometimes self-contradictory and internally irreconcilable notion which is variously manifested in plural (though inseparable) cultural discourses – economic, ethical, legal, popular, religious, and so forth. My objective is neither to undertake *a* critique of property nor to construct a theory, but rather – using a variety of methods or media – to construct a composite picture, a collage, of property. This is not by any means a realistic or representative picture: it is more impressionistic in some of the links which it creates and leaves many blank spaces to be filled by scholars with more detailed knowledge than I can claim.

More specifically, I focus upon three dimensions of what I would call a 'cultural matrix' of the Western liberal understanding of property – first, the symbols and meanings of property in a broad cultural context; second, the histories (legal, political, social) of property; and third, the theories of property, in particular those theories which have been influential in shaping key aspects of Western liberal ideas about property. 'Meanings', 'Histories', and 'Theories' are the subjects of Chapters 2, 3, and 4 respectively. These chapters present an immanent description and critique of property theory – that is, taking the idea of property as a fundamental part of the Western and in particular liberal world-view, the approach is to explain theoretical perspectives on property, and to apply various critical techniques which contest, complicate, or challenge some core ideas about property. Chapter 5, 'Horizons', is different in that it presents in outline some alternative ways of thinking about the relationship of individuals and social groups to the world's resources: while most of these still originate in the West, they represent efforts to move beyond both traditional and critical articulations. The chapter looks at alternative theories about property, as well as contemporary activist movements which attempt to mobilise one or more of these alternatives.

Given the length of this book, I do not attempt to be comprehensive in my coverage of any of these matters. Moreover, given its introductory nature, I have endeavoured to consider a broad range of topics: even if the treatment of these is often sketchy, this seemed preferable to very detailed consideration of a more limited number of subjects. Having said that, in many respects the selection of materials and topics is a personal one, and it undoubtedly presents a very partial view of property: I touch very little, for instance, on classical economic theories about property, have hardly given credit to several important contemporary theorists such as Nozick or Rawls, and consider little of the extensive theory concerning distributive justice. More significantly for a supposedly critical approach, I have provided no systematic discussion of the extensive social-scientific scholarship which deals with the complex modalities through which things and spaces are constructed, normalised, and contested in human relationships (for some interesting examples see Pottage and Mundy 2004 (critical anthropology); Cooper 2004: 16–29; Crabtree 2006; Blomley 2004 (critical geography)).

This chapter will address a number of introductory issues. First, it will outline the approach of the book and in particular consider what a 'critical' approach is, emphasising the Kantian and Frankfurt School notions of 'critique' and extended contemporary versions of critique which address structures of power such as race, gender, class. Second, it will highlight some of the practical issues and key themes which make property such a significant part of the political and social fabric of contemporary cultures: the tension between property and the commons; debate concerning the nature of property (as a bundle of rights or as something more solid); the question of whether property is merely a legal construct or exists in some 'natural' state; and finally – most significantly for any discussion of this topic – the relationship between property and power. Third, it will outline one of these central issues in more detail – debate over the legal characterisation of property. The other themes will be considered substantially in Chapters 2, 3, and 4.

CRITICAL THEORY

This book has been specifically written as part of a series on 'critical approaches' to law. What does it mean to say that a 'critical' approach is being taken to a subject area? Why do we (legal scholars) characterise some types of scholarship as 'critical' and others as 'non-critical' or traditional? The epithet 'critical' is very frequently and self-consciously adopted by theorists who wish to distinguish their style, method, or approach from 'non-critical' or 'traditional' scholarship. The same cannot be said of those we (critical scholars) designate as 'non-critical': hardly anyone characterises their own scholarship as 'non-critical' or 'traditional' (Pavlich 2005: 95–6; Douzinas 2005: 47), though many have positioned themselves in opposition to particular forms of critique. Indeed, shouldn't all scholarship aspire to be 'critical' in the sense that it ought to refuse to take accepted knowledge at face value? Surely it is the task of scholarship to be self-reflective as well as to subject others' views to detailed scrutiny in the interests of promoting debate and dialogue. Self-designated 'critics' do not 'own' critique any more than I 'own' property by writing a book about it – unless and until of course such a claim is recognised by the community of scholars as a valid appropriation.

Interestingly, property or 'the proper' is sometimes itself deployed as a trope for that in knowledge which is established, bounded or obviously correct. By contrast, critique would be the improper or non-proprietorial. Consider this tantalising thought from Julia Chryssostalis and Patricia Tuitt:

> For critique, there can be no hope or promise of closure: it is fated to occupy that enduring state of anxiety that accompanies the homeless, the wayward or the dispossessed.
>
> (2005: 1)

Established knowledge has closure or at least aims for it, even if this is by way of an artificially enforced boundary or set of undisclosed or unexamined assumptions. Critical theory is destined to be constantly 'on the move', unlike the owner but like the dispossessed. This metaphor works only while property is regarded as an exclusive and closed terrain: it becomes more difficult to sustain once we start thinking that perhaps property is itself not proper, closed, or certain. (I will come back to this in Chapter 2.)

As usual, I am getting ahead of myself. To return to the question, what is a *critical* approach, which would be different from a normal scholarly approach? Critical theory, as understood by contemporary critical legal scholars, can mean a number of different things. Reference is often made to the philosopher Immanuel Kant, whose critical works – primarily the critiques of *Pure Reason*, *Practical Reason* and *Judgment* – were generated by the need to establish secure non-dogmatic foundations for knowledge. In this sense, critique is the necessary and a priori basis of all that we know: without it, we simply have assumptions and beliefs (Kant 1929: 9). Critique is also often understood as social critique, consisting of a more expressly socio-political agenda of systematically exposing the operations of power and domination in ordinary social structures and institutions in order to change them: such a form of critique may be traced to Marx (1845). In its twentieth-century form, Max Horkheimer reiterated Marx's call for a transformative social critique and argued that critical theory is immanent and reflexive: it is immanent because rather than simply rejecting a particular system of established thought from the outside, it works at finding the internal contradictions and inconsistencies of that theory; critique is also reflexive in that it appreciates the interrelationship of objects, theories and subjects in the process of knowledge construction (Horkheimer 1972: 2010–211).

In the more specifically legal tradition (though as others have pointed out, there is a legal element of philosophical critique[2]), although the US-based critical legal studies movement was the first self-consciously to adopt the term, 'critical' legal scholarship is now geographically widespread and diffuse in its themes and approaches (Douzinas and Geary 2005: 229–58). Legal critique can be either abstract/conceptual or social/transformative or, ideally, both: the forms of critique which have most successfully connected the abstract and the practical are those strongly motivated by the need to transform social distributions of power – feminism, critical race theory, critiques of ongoing colonialism and imperialism within law, sexuality and gender critiques. All of these critical approaches have had an impact on property theory, some aspects of which will be considered throughout the book.

Referring to the critical approaches of Kant (epistemological critique) and Marx (social critique), Wacquant argues that a combination of both is to be preferred:

> . . . the most fruitful critical thought is that which . . . weds epistemological and social critique by questioning, in a continuous, active, and radical manner, both established forms of thought and established collective life – 'common sense' or *doxa* (including the *doxa* of the critical tradition) along with the social and political relations that obtain at a particular moment in a particular society.
>
> (2004: 97)

If I were to adopt a manifesto for the book, then, this would be it: to combine the epistemological and fundamental critical analysis of the concepts, theories, and established knowledge about property with an understanding of the social and political conditions of property distribution which co-exist with these concepts. Property is an exceptionally fertile ground for such critique, since – as many have observed – its very being is often predicated upon the liberal ideal of individual human self-determination, and yet its existence is also the foundation of inequality and of an inability to determine one's own destiny. Property both represents and destroys the individual and her rights. It is empowering and enabling for the proprietor, but often disempowering and disabling for non-proprietors. Its characteristics as a vehicle of inequality are only too evident, though its enabling effects are also apparent. Moreover, the inequality associated with property is not randomly distributed, but distributed systemically alongside other axes of social differentiation such as race and gender. At the same time, property itself provides some means of resistance to vested capitalist interests, for instance through the Lockean notion of inalienable self-ownership. Some activist and philosophical means of resisting the inequalities of property are considered further in Chapter 5.

As I will explain, property is also a powerful metaphor for existence in a liberal social framework – its reach is not only material and political, but also cultural and symbolic. Here again, we see a systemically unequal distribution of symbolic 'capital' or 'cultural property' (Skeggs 2004): to take only the most well-known and obvious example, women's sexuality has often been commodified within a heteronormative culture, making women more recognisable as objects than as owners. Whiteness can also be seen as a form of property – valuable, territorial, and often mapped onto physical landscapes (Harris 1993). I will come back to this, and other similar themes, in Chapter 2.

Property, then, is highly susceptible to critique and yet, to my way of thinking, it is an area of legal and political thought where the boundaries between established and critical positions are not entirely clear cut. In a way which may not be true of ordinary legal theory, the history of property theory is in a sense a history of social, if not always epistemological, critique. For instance, John Locke might today be regarded as the champion of neo-liberal individualist approaches to property as well as an apologist for the expropriation of Indigenous lands through colonial expansion. Yet his thinking was based on what was in his day the rather radical anti-feudal notion that people naturally own themselves and their labour. His theory was redistributive, both of political and proprietary rights. Moreover, much twentieth-century property theory took place, either explicitly or implicitly, in the shadow of Marx's social critique and transformative praxis. And even the more conceptual legal-analytical property theory has, for the better part of a century, been preoccupied with some fundamental critical questions about the nature of property – does it exist as a distinct legal category, or is it just a particularly strong concentration of otherwise common legal rights and obligations (Hohfeld 1913; 1917; Penner 1997)? Is property really 'proper' (that is, self-contained and distinct), or is it 'dis-integrated' or 'fragmented'? Does it have a stable identity or is it dynamic and mutable? Such issues are hardly radical in mainstream property theory, though they do provide an opening for debate about the economic and distributional consequences of different conceptions of property.

There are, of course, many perspectives on property which could be characterised as 'established' or 'traditional': for instance, liberal and libertarian conceptions which see property as essentially indi-vidual and inviolable, as a natural legal right, and as a necessary mechanism for protection of the person against a hostile social environment and state (Gaus 1994). Economic accounts of property which feed into the highly mobile practices of advanced capitalism are likely to see it as less absolute and intrinsically tradable, while encouraging the commodification of more resources. While such extreme economic approaches, which may also reduce all rights into alienable property, contest the more solid classical liberal view, they have little in common with critical accounts concerned (in part) to highlight the political and social consequences of non-critical economics.

Popular struggles concerning property often manifest a conflict between established conceptions of property and critical ideas (see generally Blomley 2004, and Chapter 5 below) – these may disrupt proprietorial modes of power, they may reinvigorate pre-liberal notions of property, they may mobilise traditional concepts of prop-erty for dissident objectives, or even prefigure an alternative mode of resource management. Compare the pastoralist wanting exclusive possession and use of a tract of land with the Indigenous com-munities who wish to be recognised as the original inhabitants and custodians of their country. Compare the rural landowner with the ramblers wishing to use an ancient right of way. Compare the bankrupt factory/shop owner with the collective of workers/buyers who wish to operate the resource for the benefit of their community. Compare the corporate producers of software or encyclopaedias with the open-source software movement, the creative commons movement, or the collaborative creation of free online encyclopaedias. Liberal law is frequently, though not always, on the side of the individual proprietor (who may or may not choose to take full advantage of that law) but alternative conceptions and practices constantly disrupt the hegemony of liberal property law. The positions are not, moreover, necessarily polarised in the way I have described them: extreme perspectives may be compromised by necessity or even by imaginative alliances between interest-bearers.

Thus, critique and resistance are embedded in much property theory as well as in the praxis of ownership, and it would be unwise to insist too much on a clear distinction between traditional and critical theory in this field. This is hardly surprising given extreme inequalities in global distributions of property: frequently this inequality seems associated with the concept of property itself, rather than political or social contingencies (though these clearly also play a part). There is therefore an inbuilt motivation to question property as a concept and an institution. At the same time, property is not a necessarily exploitative institution. A recent collection of essays illustrates that the reduction of things to fungible property, or commodification, is a socially and politically ambiguous phenomenon: as Carol Rose puts it, the market has an 'enormous potential for experiment and novelty' (Rose 2005, 417; see generally Ertman and Williams 2005).

SIGNIFICANCE OF PROPERTY: SOME KEY THEMES

Although I have broadly divided the book into this introduction, followed by chapters on the meanings, histories, theories and (new) horizons of property, these are not at all distinct areas of analysis. One of the core points I wish to convey is that property cannot be understood merely as a legal concept, or as a set of cultural meanings, or in the context of philosophical theories. Like many other culturally loaded terms, property is at once a very dense idea, full of resonance in many fields, as well as one which is extraordinarily slippery. Even if I believed in the possibility and utility of 'grand theory' or 'metanarrative' (which I do not), an interdisciplinary account of property is definitely one area where such an enquiry would be destined to ridiculous failure. There are too many contradictions and contested meanings, too many loose ends, too much contingency and arbitrariness, too many insecure and constructed subject-positions, mixed in with the order, the certainty, the predictability, and the solidity of (certain aspects of) property. This is not, I hasten to add, a negative reflection on the many excellent attempts at describing, justifying, and analysing property: these theories, however, tend to focus upon one dimension of property – law, political theory, or moral philosophy. In the tradition of other critical property theorists in the Anglosphere, my approach is more partial, and more intent on both describing and unravelling key ideas about property.

Cutting across the core building blocks of meaning, history and theory are a number of motifs which recur throughout virtually any discussion of property. Indeed, perhaps these are not just themes which keep coming up *within* property analysis – perhaps these issues are rather together *constitutive* of 'our' (Western) notion of property. Perhaps much property theory is no more than a particular positioning within the debates generated by these defining issues. I will outline each of these motifs briefly: most of them will arise repeatedly throughout the book.

Liberal conception of property

Several of these key themes – the public/private distinction, the 'possessive individual', property as providing protection from the state – coalesce around the political theory of liberalism. For liberal thought, property is central to the constitution of the citizen as a political actor within a democratic polity. It has been seen as delineating the private sphere as a separate zone from the public, and it protects citizens from state interference, providing a space of private resistance against a potentially antagonistic and intrusive state. It is characteristic of liberalism to think of the state as at best in tension with the individual or at worst her enemy, whereas more communally oriented and social democratic political ideologies are more likely to construct the state as the friend or 'home' of the community (Svensson and Pylkkänen 2004: 17–18; Gunnarsson et al. 2004: 137–8). In this context, property, together with other legally reified individual rights, is traditionally seen as inviolable, and as providing protection for the individual *against* the state and against a 'tyran-nical democratic majority' which 'confers on people the independ-ence necessary for proper citizenship' (McLean 1999b: 1). Property strengthens liberal individualism. Moreover, the liberal concept of property privatises the power associated with it: people are regarded as equally free, equally able to accumulate (subject to opportunity), and differentiated in private by their property. At the same time, in the public sphere, these differentiations are, according to liberal thought, made irrelevant by virtue of the equality of citizens as polit-ical actors. The political power of property is therefore erased by the public/private distinction.

The critique of property as a construction of liberal legal culture therefore emphasises its significance to the public/private distinction, its role in constituting and strengthening the liberal individual, and its role as private counterweight to state power. Because property is sometimes seen as coextensive with liberty and democracy, any cri-tique of property in this extreme liberal form can be seen as a threat to individual liberty and a threat to democratic institutions. Having said that, law certainly does not simply reflect the liberal-capitalist ideal of property: it is infinitely more complicated in its constructions of a dynamic social, economic, and political environment.

The distinction between public and private, for instance, is not a bright line. Clearly, for instance, private property only exists insofar as it is publicly acknowledged through the institution of law (Frey-fogle 2006). Any space may be subject to plural meanings or appropri-ations which do not necessarily come into conflict: pastoralists and Indigenous people may have quite different understandings of rural landscapes reflected in different types of property interests, which can – ideally – coexist legally. A nominally open public space may have 'private' or limited meanings imposed upon it – for instance religious meanings (see Cooper 2004: 16ff.). Urban spaces such as privately owned but publicly accessible shopping malls are increasingly of a 'quasi'-public nature (Gray and Gray 1999; cf. Bottomley 2007). At the same time, intrusions of public norms into personal proprietary spaces through, for instance, zoning, heritage, and environmental regulations, militate against seeing 'private' property as entirely pri-vate. Social transitions which transgress neat liberal distinctions put the theory under strain in key points: where the owners of a quasi-public space like a shopping mall try to enforce a dress code or standards of behaviour, private proprietorial power intrudes into the public sphere (See generally McLean 1999a; Bottomley 2007).

More generally, contemporary philosophy has also raised a number of critical questions concerning the 'subject' or autonomous human entity which is the foundation for liberal thought. Autonomous individuals are naturalised in liberal thought, a position which has been challenged by theorists who see subjects as more plural, hybrid, post-social and contextual. The critique of subjectivity, as I will explain towards the end of Chapter 4, may hold possibilities for reconceptualising property as a relationship which connects rather than divides people.

Propriety and the proper

A second theme, very much associated with the first, is the association of property with class status. In Chapter 3 I outline some of the ways in which property and political standing were formally connected in the past: for instance, through property restrictions on suffrage. However, even though such formal associations are a thing of the past, the idea that property is there to reflect and cement propriety – the proper order of the social and political spheres – still carries a strong resonance. In relation to US 'takings' law,[3] Carol Rose puts it like this:

> What is the purpose of property under this . . . understanding? The purpose is to accord to each person or entity what is 'proper' or 'appropriate' to him or her. Indeed, this understanding of property historically made no strong distinction between 'property' and 'propriety', and one finds the terminology mixed up to a very considerable degree in historical texts. And what is 'proper' or appropriate, on this vision of property, is that which is needed to keep good order in the commonwealth or body politic.
>
> (Rose 1994: 58)

As Rose explains, this notion of the propriety of property and its role in stabilising the political order takes us back at least to feudal times, where political status and authority had to do with family heritage, position in a hierarchy of landholdings, and inalienable connection to a (generally) male-controlled estate. Even though feudalism in its English form has been dying for the past 800 years or so, it is not yet dead and, moreover, the social distinctions which it fostered and the centrality it placed upon certain forms of property remain in circulation in many spheres of existence. It is, for example, reflected in a traditional 'stately homes' understanding of heritage law – a law which protects the cultural property of elites to the exclusion of more popular, pluralistic or alternative values (Petrie 2005; English 2007). I will come back to the increasingly democratised understandings of heritage, which emphasise a social 'ownership' of certain spaces and cultural resources, in Chapter 5.

Beyond the determination of one's proper place in a hierarchical social order, I argue in Chapter 2 that the metaphors of the proper and propriety serve a far broader purpose in defining and shaping notions of identity, law, and epistemological categories. In this sense property as propriety enters further into the construction of social identity than simply being about what we own: regardless of whether we are owners, the notion of property, with its boundaries and exclusion zones, helps to define 'me' and 'you' within the liberal cultural context. It therefore defines symbolic and cultural capital, placing people within notional – but socially significant – hierarchies (Skeggs 2004; Petrie 2005; Blackstone 2005).

Subjects and objects of property

Kantian philosophy distinguishes between entities which are moral 'ends in themselves' and entities which are only means (Kant 1988: 273). This distinction essentially maps onto the contemporary Western distinction between persons and property or subjects and objects of ownership. Persons are legal subjects and as such are moral ends. They can own property and – leaving aside artificial legal persons such as corporations – they are not property. In times and jurisdictions where slavery was recognised, the distinction between (human) persons and property did not hold: under those conditions, some persons were legally regarded as means rather than ends, property rather than person.

The modern person–property/subject–object distinction seems relatively straightforward, but it is complicated and undermined by several factors (see generally Davies and Naffine 2001). For instance, from an analytical point of view, and as I will explain in more detail shortly, property is not an object at all, but rather a legally defined relationship between persons with respect to an object. 'Property' is only an effect, a construction, of relationships between people, meaning that its objective character is contestable. Persons and things, as a recent collection of anthropological essays makes clear,

are 'constituted' or 'fabricated' by legal and other normative techniques (Pottage and Mundy 2004). Alternative constructions of
property, such as the notion of stewardship, may challenge the
subject–object and person–property distinctions. Moreover, within
liberal philosophy, the person is often construed as a self-owning
entity – the 'possessive individual' as MacPherson termed it (1964).
The person is both subject and object of her own property, existing
as a self-relation which is divided and yet whole, for instance as
(owning) mind and (owned) body. Finally, at the very practical level,
there are arguably numbers of ways in which the person–property
distinction is transgressed within the law: in some jurisdictions of the
United States, personality rights allow the persona to be packaged
and sold as an object of intellectual property (Dangelo 1989);
human DNA has been patented (Barrad 1993); some body parts, in
some parts of the world, can be legally sold (Nwabueze 2002).
Chapter 3 contains further consideration of this issue.

Proper and common

Once again related to all of the above is the fact that property is most
often constructed as *private* property, meaning that the associated
rights vest in an individual (or a corporate entity). Private property is
often seen as an efficient form of resource control, in contrast to
common and public ownership, which is seen as potentially wasteful
and possibly leading to overuse and degradation (Hardin 1968).
Moreover, within the liberal context the private nature of property is
naturalised and universalised, as though other forms are somehow
less ethically defensible. (For instance, it is sometimes claimed that
communal ownership would negate the rights of individuals.) Social
contestations of various types of enclosure and privatisation are
framed around ideological, ethical, and political disputes about what
types of resources and opportunities ought to be freely available, or
at least available to limited communities. Recently, for instance,
scholars have written extensively about the encroachment of intellectual property rights into the public domain. Some of these practical
issues will be dealt with in Chapter 3.

The relationship of property to the commons extends further than
practical issues of which resources should be available to all, and
which can be privately owned. In some cases contemporary claims of
property are more about what Murphy, Roberts and Flessas refer to
as 'symbolic networks' – the meanings which circulate through

cultures about certain items or resources (Murphy et al 2004: 28). Like many concepts derived from Western political philosophy, the liberal-individualist notion of private property is often assumed to be universal or definitive of property on a global scale. As I will explain in Chapter 4, it was complicit in colonial appropriations of territory from those who defined their relationships to land differently. In the post-colonial world, neo-liberal constructions and distributions of property are often associated with Western imperialism, enabling, for instance, the mining or 'prospecting' of majority world and Indigenous cultures, peoples, and antiquities as though they were natural resources (Shiva 1997; 2001; Mgbeoji 2006).

The term 'cultural' property has become popular as a way of designating the distinctive cultural resources, 'symbolic networks' and identity of different peoples: because it belongs to groups, it is a form of property which is common rather than private. 'Cultural appropriation' is the morally (though not often legally) dubious practice whereby (usually) outside entrepreneurs turn cultural resources into economically valuable commodities. Such cultural appropriation might consist of the removal of a valuable antiquity for sale to private collectors or to European or North American museums. (Such takings are now highly regulated, but also represent an area where illicit trade is common.) Cultural appropriation may also take the form of white artists using the motifs and styles of Indigenous artists in order to create saleable artworks, or of pharmaceutical companies isolating and patenting the useful ingredients of traditional medicines (Shiva 1997). Of course, cultural property does not only belong to a vast non-European other, and cultural appropriation does not only refer to takings by Western actors from non-Western sites. One of the most celebrated cases of appropriation of cultural property concerns the dispute over the Parthenon (Elgin) marbles removed from Greece in the nineteenth century and currently held – allegedly on behalf of humanity – in the British Museum (Murphy et al 2004: 29–30). In this dispute the alleged cultural identity of the Greek people is pitted against the supposed cultural heritage of the entire world population.

Property as natural right or positive construct

Much property theory concerns the application of natural law and positivist approaches: does property have an existence independent

of law, or is it entirely a legal construct? A strong natural law tradition in the history of property theory sees property as something
objective: either it exists in some presumed 'state of nature' or its
existence is justified and delineated from natural reason (see generally Christman 1986). On this view, the role of the law is to protect
something which pre-exists any legal recognition and is not only
conventional, much as human rights law is sometimes said to protect
rights which people have simply because of their human status (and
not as constructed by law). This debate raises issues for the definition
of property: if a local council puts a historically significant house on
a heritage register, imposes zoning restrictions or refuses a request to
cut down a significant tree, is it interfering with the house-owner's
(natural) property rights, or simply re-adjusting the legal property
rights the owner has in the house? If we have natural property rights,
the shape of those rights must also to some degree be natural.

Personally I have never been fond of natural law arguments (see
Davies 2002b, 79–86). The natural-rights sceptic Jeremy Bentham
stated that 'property and law are born together and die together'
(Bentham 1931: 113; cf. Cohen 1954, 371–3). From this point of
view, property is created by law, rather than recognised by law. Whatever law says is or can be property defines the limits of property: it
does not pre-exist law, but is entirely defined within law. The anarchist Proudhon also raised against property a familiar objection to
natural law:

> If property is a natural, absolute, imprescriptible, and inalienable
> right, why, in all ages, has there been so much preoccupation with
> its origin? For this is one of its distinguishing characteristics. The
> origin of a natural right: Good God, whoever inquired into the
> origin of the rights of liberty, security, or equality?
>
> (Proudhon 1994: 43)

A natural right ought to be self-evident and it ought to be universal.
There should not be hundreds of different views about what it consists of. Even supposing there is a natural right, the fact that there are
different interpretations of it render the supposition irrelevant – we
may as well get on with debating the content of 'right' without reference to whether it is natural or not. In fact, such sceptical arguments
apply not just to property but to any claimed natural right. What is
'natural' generally turns out to be very much in the eye of the
beholder in her or his cultural, religious, or political context. The

other rights Proudhon mentions – liberty, security, and equality – are no more natural than the right to property. The conclusion is frequently, but mistakenly, reached that because there are no natural moral norms, therefore there are no moral norms. But a rejection of natural law does not entail the rejection of morality. Rather, the question is really not where such norms come from, but rather how we humans want to construct the basis of our co-existence.

From a critical perspective it is of course highly simplistic to suppose that the theoretical possibilities are covered by natural law or positivism. As I have suggested, the so-called 'natural' domain is as much a political and cultural construct as the domain of law: this does not mean that positivist arguments are correct (though in my view they do have more credibility than arguments based on some pre-social, rational or universal condition). In particular, the broad critical approach I adopt in this book regards positive law as conceptually plural, inseparable from social environments, and liable to be contested from both an internal and an external perspective (and indeed, contested in its construction of internal and external spheres). On this view, property does not have a natural or essential form, but nor is it entirely defined by law in the narrow positivist sense: property is itself plural, contestable, dynamic, and shaped by a multitude of legal and other discourses.

Property as a legal construct

If property is not a natural moral norm protecting some pre-social relationship a person has with a thing, if it is entirely a legal construct, then the question often arises as to what kind of legal concept it is. Does it have a special status in that it can be distinguished clearly from other parts of the law, and does it have a coherent form which can be expressed as a clear set of principles? On the other hand, is it just a convenient term for a range of legal rights which are not especially distinct but which tend to congeal around certain types of legal relationships? I will have more to say about this particular issue at the end of this chapter so will not pursue it further here.

Except to make one point: Kevin Gray has suggested that property is an illusion – not a meaningless figment of the imagination, but rather an object of desire through which we are 'seduced into believing that we have found an objective reality which embodies our intuitions and needs' (1991: 252; cf. Cohen 1954). Understanding the social power of property as a myth which is not just a legal fiction but also a collective ideal, fantasy, or desire, is integral to legal, philosophical, and more socially oriented critiques. Saying that property is a myth or fiction does not imply that it does not exist: rather, it is a construction which we believe in, with very significant social and legal effects. Whatever the position of law, and regardless of how property is constructed within law, this legal myth or fiction of property exists in tension with broader social norms and cultural meanings. While it is certainly possible and valuable to focus upon distinctive legal constructions of property, the critical context is far broader and in the end inseparable from law, as I will endeavour to illustrate.

Property and power

Perhaps most importantly for a book emphasising critical approaches is the association of property with various forms of power. As I indicated briefly above, the liberal conception of property essentially privatises the power associated with property – it insists, like Roman law, on a distinction between *imperium*, or political power, and *dominium*, or private power. The distinction will be questioned in a variety of ways throughout the book: for the moment it suffices to quote Morris Cohen's enduring soundbite: 'we must not overlook the actual fact that *dominion* over things is also *imperium* over our fellow human beings' (Cohen, 1927: 13). Property, in other words, is not just about our power over an object; it is fundamentally about our ability to exclude others from a resource: exclusion and the exercise of power are, of course, intimately related.

CONCEPTS OF PROPERTY

How is property understood conceptually by common law theorists? In this section, I introduce briefly some issues which provide a sort of conceptual toolkit for later chapters. It is sometimes said that property is suffering an identity crisis. James Penner, personifying property, put it like this:

> 'You see', property will say, 'now I am not even my own idea. I'm just a bundle of other concepts, a mere chimera of an entity. I'm just a quivering, wavering, normative phantasm, without any

home, without anything to call my own but an album full of fading and tattered images of vitality and consequence and meaning. I'm depressed.'

(Penner 1997: 1)

Property appears to be much more of a floating signifier than it used to be, more vague, more able to attach to a variety of different legal relationships. It has lost its solid, reassuring, conceptual distinctiveness. Of course, to state that a concept or institution is in crisis does not necessarily signal a decline, but may rather indicate more of a reorientation, an expansion, a reconsideration, reconstruction – certainly containing a negative moment, but not necessarily a destructive one. The rights afforded by property are said to be no longer absolutely distinguishable from those offered by other legal categories, property no longer carries an essential set of incidents, and it governs our relationships to an increasingly complicated and abstract set of objects.

Technically speaking, as far as the common law is concerned, 'property' does not refer to a class of things, but rather to a type of relationship between persons with respect to things. It is true that 'property' is frequently used as a shorthand method of referring to a thing which is owned but, as Jeremy Bentham explained 200 years ago, 'in common speech in the phrase *the object of a man's property*, the words *the object of* are commonly left out' (Bentham 1970: chapter XVI, s 26, n 1). Thus when we refer to an object as 'property', we are forgetting that the 'property' is not the object itself, but rather a legal category which gives a person certain rights over the object.

Common law theorists have debated the nature of property extensively. In the twentieth century, part of the debate about the nature of property concerned a seemingly dry issue: does 'property' denote an analytically distinct legal right or is it just a convenient way of referring to a bundle of rights which will vary according to the context? Is property essentially a distinct power over objects and over other people, or is it a more dispersed and contextual set of rights? Drawing upon the definitions mentioned above, we might ask, is property proper? Or is it just common, like contract? (cf. Penner 1997: 1)

The extremities of opinion can be quite simply demonstrated, even though there are many complexities which I do not have space to consider here. At one extreme, there are the words of William Blackstone which I quoted at the beginning of this chapter: property is 'the sole and despotic dominion which one man claims and exercises over the external things of the world in total exclusion of the right of any other individual in the universe'. There are two interesting dimensions of this much-quoted statement. First, it characterises property in absolute terms. Property is presented as absolute domination of external things and total exclusion of others from any control over the use to which such property is put. It is a relationship of control, both over a thing and over others who may wish to make use of the thing. Second, the implication is that property actually precedes the protection of property by law. Instead of regarding property merely as a construction of law, it is regarded as something which 'one man claims and exercises'. As we saw, Blackstone also voiced doubt over the legitimacy and absoluteness of the concept, but his opening statement nonetheless represents one extreme – the concept of property as 'despotic dominion' over things.

In contrast to Blackstone's evocation of a very strong idea of property, twentieth-century theorists have 'disaggregated' the notion of property (Grey 1980). Instead of thinking of property as having some special and distinctive character that precedes legal protection, positivist and realist thinkers have argued that property is no different from other legal categories, in that it is simply a consequence of the significance attached *by law* to the relationships between legal persons. Property is not in essence a special relationship between a person and a thing. This was most famously suggested by the American jurist Wesley Newcombe Hohfeld, who essentially argued that the distinction between rights *in rem* (against the world) and rights *in personam* (against a person)[4] does not consist in a qualitative difference in the type of right, but rather a difference in the scope or degree of application of the right (Hohfeld 1917: 718–22, 745). Put simply, the difference between property and contract or other types of legal obligations, on this view, is that property gives rise to a multitude of rights and correlative duties, whereas rights arising under a contract are confined to the parties.

Opinion in twentieth-century common law theory has tended to favour the view that property is not essentially a 'right to a thing', but rather a separable bundle of rights subsisting between persons which may vary according to the context and the object which is at stake. Such rights traditionally include the right to use, abuse, alienate, and exclude others (Honoré 1961; Becker 1980; cf. Pottage 1998). 'Property' has no essential character, but is rather a highly flexible set of rights and responsibilities which congeal in different ways in different contexts (Grey 1980; cf. Gray 1991; Underkuffler 1990). Legally, property is not proper, that is, it has no special, distinct, and essential characteristics. It is more or less a concept in circulation, which changes according to the context in which it finds itself. Increasingly, property is also regarded as consisting of both rights and obligations: property concerns not only the individual as proprietor, but also the communities within which it exists (Singer 2000; Raff 1998).

As some have argued, the 'disaggregation' of property – that is, the movement away from a view of property as a natural and inviolable dominance over a thing – might just make the whole concept of property more flexible, meaning that an increasing range of things can become property (Schroeder 1994a: 243–4; Edgeworth 1988: 98). If property is not a definite set of rights (such as the right to exclude others, the right to use and enjoy, the right to transfer, the right to destroy) but includes different rights for different contexts, then maybe more resources can fall within the concept of property. Indeed capitalism tends to promote the commodity form: where something can be made into an object of property, it will be. The common law can be rather flexible in allowing commodification, and also encourages the legal fragmentation of property into increasingly small parts (Heller 1999). Thus the bundle of rights picture of property may promote the commodification of a larger number of things. At the same time, the denaturalisation of property and the movement away from seeing property as an absolute right, arguably provides the space in which property can develop into a more socially responsive concept (Singer 2000; cf. Caldwell 1986).

CONCLUSION

The structure of property as understood by post-Hohfeldian property theorists is rather like the structure of subjectivity or the structure of meaning as understood by post-modern theorists: it is an *effect* of relationships, or of a system of signs, not an already-existent category, and less still a unique bond between intentional being and thing from which certain consequences ideally flow. However, the so-called identity crisis of property is itself an ambiguous and politically indeterminate phenomenon: it may signal the death of property rights, or the death of a unique and individuated concept of property (Grey 1980), or recognition of the mythical, illusory, and entirely constructed nature of a property right (Cohen 1935: 816–18), or fragmentation and expansion in the objects which can become property (Heller 1999), or the uncontrollable dissemination of property as idea, metaphor, and legal relationship. At the same time, as I have indicated above, the legal characterisation of property co-exists with a more naturalistic, popular, and absolute conception. Strategic or political contexts may call for a choice to be made between these differing conceptions.

The following chapters attempt to draw out a number of other variables in the symbolic, historical, and theoretical dimensions of property. As I indicated at the outset, my aim is not to contain or unify property as an idea. Rather, my objective is to outline some of the normal and normative resonances of property, while giving an impression of how plural and contradictory it can be.

Notes

1 That is, the property theory of English-speaking common law countries where recognition of Indigenous law is wholly or at least largely on the terms dictated by the dominant legal system. I will frequently use the terms 'the West' or 'Western liberal' as a shorthand to refer to views or positions which arose primarily in parts of Western Europe, the English colonies, and (later) the colonial successor states, but which have become more geographically widespread. My focus is on the Anglo-American versions of these views, especially when I refer to forms of liberalism.

2 See Douzinas 2005: 48–51, commenting on Gillian Rose 1984, commenting on Kant 1929: 9. Kant's passage is worth repeating: 'It is obviously the effect not of levity but of the matured judgment of the age, which refuses to be any longer put off with illusory knowledge. It is a call to reason to undertake anew the most difficult of all its tasks, namely, that of self-knowledge, and to institute a tribunal which will assure to reason its lawful claims, and dismiss all groundless pretensions, not by despotic decrees, but in accordance with its own eternal and unalterable laws. This tribunal is no other than the *critique of pure reason*.' (Emphasis in original.)

3 'Takings' law refers to the body of jurisprudence developed under the Takings Clause of the Fifth Amendment of the US Constitution. This clause governs the conditions on which government may appropriate private property.

4 The term 'rights *in rem*' essentially refers to rights exercisable against the world at large. Rights *in rem* are traditionally associated with property rights, but the term also applies to (for instance) a person's right to bodily autonomy. Rights *in personam*, in contrast, are rights exercisable in relation to a more limited group – for instance the rights under a contract. However, there are variations on how the distinction is understood (Hohfeld 1917: 714; Eleftheriadis 1996: 41–7).

Chapter 2

Meanings

What then is truth? A mobile army of metaphors, metonyms, and anthropomorphisms – in short, a sum of human relations, which have been enhanced, transposed, and embellished poetically and rhetorically, and which after long use seem firm, canonical, and obligatory to a people: truths are illusions about which one has forgotten that this is what they are; metaphors which are worn out and without sensuous power; coins which have lost their pictures and now matter only as metal, no longer as coins.

(Nietzsche 1954a: 47)

INTRODUCTION

How would you perceive yourself if you did not think that you were an independent mind controlling your own thoughts inside an individual, skin-limited body?[1] What sense would you have of yourself if you did not have clear boundaries to your being? What if you experienced yourself through an array of emotions, relationships and states of mind which did not uniquely emanate from you or belong to you, but were things existing in your community and your world? You would exist, but how would you represent yourself? What if, at the same time, law did not have its concepts of jurisdiction, geographical terrain, sovereignty, and separation from the social field? Would it be law if we could identify no distinct boundaries to the concept? And furthermore, what would knowledge be without the separation of knowing subjects from known objects? What if there were no closed categories of thought, disciplines, or frameworks of understanding?

What if the metaphor of property did not shape our world? What world would we then inhabit?

In posing these perhaps provocative questions I do not intend to imply either that the Western world can do without the metaphor (or practice) of property or, on the other hand, that Western culture is entirely determined by it. However, the objective of this chapter is to illustrate that the cultural resonance and political effects of property extend far beyond its formal legal existence. Thinking about property as a metaphor is important for several reasons. As I have implied in the opening paragraph, some of the foundations of Western culture share characteristics with the idea of property and may even be said to be defined through the metaphor of property. At the same time, many of these meanings, for instance the concept of the self-contained individual, feed back into and reinforce the dominant conceptions of property understood in its 'proper' sense as a relationship between persons and things. As Bradley Bryan has pointed out, property is about much more than a set of legal relations: it is 'an expression of social relationships because it organizes people with respect to each other and their material environment' (Bryan 2000: 4).

This chapter will consider some of the ways in which the idea of property affects knowledge, social interactions, notions of law, and concepts of the self. While some of the questions raised here may seem remote from the philosophical and (especially) the legal notion of property, I aim, in this chapter, to consider the social and philosophical reach of property as an idea, and also to establish some of its structural characteristics. In this sense, the chapter deals with the ontology of property, basically, what its existence consists of in the Western liberal cultural context. In emphasising this issue, I identify certain dominant meanings or expressions of property, but this should not be taken to imply that property has a single meaning or can be reduced to a core semiotic conflict. In fact, as I hope to show, I see property as a highly contested concept with a range of possible constructions according to different contexts. I start abstractly, with a conceptual discussion, but will relate this later in the chapter to some more practical issues.

The metaphysical concept of 'the proper', a construct embedded in language and knowledge, which has been identified and critiqued by Jacques Derrida, is of particular significance here (Derrida 1974: 26). The 'proper' brings together a matrix of values, such as purity, self-identity, and exclusivity, which are reiterated in various cultural forms. For instance, as I will explain, C.B. MacPherson's famous discussion of the 'possessive individual' shows how Western culture constructs human beings as forms of self-owning property, bringing together the legally separate forms of property and the person, or object and subject (MacPherson 1964). In turn, the possessive individual, in some forms of property-theory, serves as a basis for justifying acquisition and control of resources. Scholars have also commented upon 'whiteness' and 'masculinity' as forms of property, with both material and cultural-symbolic implications (Harris 1993; Nedelsky 1990). The chapter will consider these and other variations on the theme of property as a culturally significant metaphor and, where appropriate, relate these meanings to the more practical questions relating to property as a form of resource management.

THE PROPER

'Property' is an extremely suggestive word, in that its broader connotations imply not only legal categories, but also certain social or cultural attitudes. An object of property is said to be 'proper' to its owner, meaning that there is a distinct and particular link between the object and its owner. Even exploring only these two related words, 'proper' and 'property', we find an amazing family of concepts centred on notions of sameness, personal autonomy, authenticity, purity, propriety, and being owned (Davies 1998).

The primary definition in the Oxford English Dictionary states that 'proper' means 'belonging to oneself or itself; (one's or its) own; owned as property; that is the, or a, property or quality of the thing itself, intrinsic, inherent'. Other meanings include 'special, particular, distinctive, characteristic', 'in conformity with rule; strict, accurate, exact', 'identical', 'genuine, true, real; regular, normal', 'thorough, complete, perfect', 'of good character or standing; honest, respectable', 'becoming, decent, decorous'. 'Proper' also simply refers to a 'private possession, private property'. Thus we see that the term 'proper', which is ordinarily associated with the *personal* qualities of propriety and respectability, also implies questions relating to ownership. The 'proper' person is the one who owns and is true to herself or himself, and is thus genuine, perfect, pure.

'Property' is also intrinsically connected with personal characteristics: not only does it refer to a thing which is owned, but also to a particular condition of a person or thing. Thus 'property' is defined as 'that which one owns', 'a peculiar or exclusive attribute', 'the quality of being proper or suitable'. There is a quality of authenticity, and erasure of difference in the name of conformity, about property and the proper, commented upon by Derrida:

> The horizon of absolute knowledge is . . . the reappropriation of difference, the accomplishment of what I have elsewhere called the *metaphysics of the proper* [*le propre* – self-possession, propriety, property, cleanliness].
>
> (Derrida 1974: 26)

As Derrida points out, a proper name is supposedly an untranslatable word which connects directly to an object – one name, one object – without engaging with the entire conceptual structure of language (Derrida 1985: 171; Bennington 1993: 104–5; cf. Davies 1998: 152). It is a vertical or hierarchical relation of name to object, which does not engage with the full horizontal contexts of language. In general, the idea of the proper indicates characteristics of territoriality, immediacy, singularity, self-possession/autonomy, legitimacy/right and purity or authenticity (Davies 1998). This notion of the proper is reflected in the idea of property as a direct relationship between a person and a thing, as opposed to the disaggregated notion of property as a dynamic set of relationships between persons (see the discussion in Chapter 1, above).

Central to any definition (some would say constitutive of it; Saussure 1959: 117; Laclau 1996: 52) is also what it excludes, its conceptual 'other'. As sovereign, right, and legitimate, the proper is defined in opposition to the improper or transgressive. As unique, pure, distinct, and immediate, it is defined in opposition to the common and the inauthentic, that which is ordinary and distributed rather than special and distinct.

It is true that the extended connotations of words – especially as presented by the nuanced definitions to be found in the Oxford English Dictionary – do not necessarily tell us anything about legal concepts, which are supposed to be precise, well defined, technical, and non-metaphorical. However, the *legal culture* of property – including the associated ideas of the proper and propriety – extends well beyond narrow and positivistic accounts of the law of property. In other words, there is a two-way relationship between legal understandings of the concept of property, and broader cultural notions of personality and the self. In addition, the predominant positivist understanding of law, and ideas of knowledge and human understanding, are also to some extent characterised through the metaphor of property.

The exact nature of the 'relationship' between property as a 'legal' idea, and these broader cultural manifestations, cannot necessarily be specified exactly, and may amount to nothing more than a certain broad conceptual similarity. Certainly I would not argue that there is a direct causal relationship between the legal concept of property and cultural uses of the idea of property. As I have explained in Chapter 1, there is a tension in the legal idea of property between seeing it as a disaggregated bundle of rights and seeing it as something more solid, specific, and identified with a particular person. In contrast, when it is used as a metaphor in a cultural and social setting, the idea of property tends towards the latter, not the former, conceptualisation. Insofar as our selves, our law, and our knowledge are defined in part through property, it is by reference to the notions of authenticity, autonomy, exclusivity and propriety.

PROPERTY AS A METAPHOR FOR SELF, LAW AND KNOWLEDGE

The proper person

In the core, practical sense with which lawyers are familiar, natural persons cannot be property. Slavery is anathema to most legal systems as is – at least formally – any arrangement which might be construed as similar to slavery. In Chapter 3, I will consider some of the practical (legal as well as extra-legal[2]) ways in which this separation of person and property is circumvented. Moreover, as I will explain in this section, the person is often constituted *symbolically* in cultural, philosophical and even legal discourse as a form of property relation.

Legal narratives about the relationship between property and personality have taken several forms (Naffine 1998: 198) of which the ideas of the philosophers G.W.F. Hegel and John Locke have been especially significant. In the first place, property ownership is said to strengthen the self by extending the line of non-interference around the person. We need to own property because it enhances our sense of self and protects us from interference by the state and by others (Hegel 1952: 41; Reich 1964, 1991; Radin 1993: 36–7). Second, the self has been defined through the idea of property: in this sense, we are said to be self-owning individuals, bounded, autonomous, and distinct. Both theories will be discussed in more detail in Chapter

4. My concern here is with the ways in which persons are said to be self-owning entities and, more broadly, to resemble property symbolically.

John Locke famously claimed that, although the resources of the world are originally owned in common, 'every Man has a *Property* in his own *Person*. This no Body has any Right to but himself' (Locke 1988: 287). As J.W. Harris remarks, liberal arguments such as Locke's are based on a 'spectacular *non sequitur*': '[f]rom the fact that nobody owns me if I am not a slave, it simply does not follow that I must own myself' (Harris 1996: 71). Despite the illogicality of the reasoning, however, the fact remains that self-ownership has significant cultural appeal and real effects, as we shall see. Private property is gained in the state of nature, according to Locke, by mixing one's labour with the things of the external world. (That one can appropriate some-thing by mixing labour with it is also dubious: Nozick 1974: 174–5). I will come back to the details of Locke's view of property in Chap-ter 4. What is of interest here is that the person is regarded as a self-owning entity; an idea commented upon nearly three centuries later by the political philosopher C.B. MacPherson:

> . . . since the freedom, and therefore the humanity, of the indi-vidual depend on his freedom to enter into self-interested rela-tions with other individuals, and since his ability to enter into such relations depends on his having exclusive control of (rights in) his own person and capacities, and since proprietorship is the generalised form of such exclusive control, the individual is essentially the proprietor of his own person and capacities.
> (MacPherson 1964: 261)

In the seventeenth-century liberal world, 'persons' were conceptual-ised as entities having 'exclusive control' over themselves, their rights, their relationships, their labour and their capacities. The possessive individual is an abstract political entity, not necessarily reflected literally in legal doctrine. Legally persons do basically have the right to control their persons and capacities – make contracts for instance. This is a personality right, not a strict legal right over ourselves as objects of property. We are legally incapable of permanently aban-doning ourselves or selling ourselves in the same way that we could abandon or sell other objects of property. According to law, persons are not property – their own or anybody else's (Harris 1996), though there may be instances where the rule is bent or discarded in favour of a more pragmatic view.[3] But MacPherson's point is more subtle than a direct application of the legal notion of property to the person. It suggests that the cultural ideology of the person in liberal societies represents the self as bounded, discrete, self-determining units. This does not mean that we *necessarily* experience ourselves exclusively in this way, though it arguably does constitute the substratum of meaning about selfhood in the West – that is, the dominant story we tell about ourselves and others, particularly in major public arenas – legal, economic, and political.

MacPherson's 'possessive individual' critiques the construction of persons by pioneering liberal-capitalist theorists. It is a conception of the self which, although 'intrinsically contestable' (Ryan 1994: 241), has had a far-reaching impact upon cultural and legal understandings of personhood. It also clearly epitomised the person as quintessentially an *owner*, a person in the seventeenth century who was almost invariably male, white, and at least upper middle class. This mode of defining the self through control over our own objectified capacities has continued into the present time. Jennifer Nedelsky, for instance, speaks of legal persons as 'bounded selves' (1990) and Beverley Skeggs argues that contemporary theoretical and popular notions of the self still draw upon possessive individualism. We (Western selves) are still conceived through the accumulation of 'cultural property' such as education, aesthetic development, and formative experiences, many of which have a cultural 'exchange value' (Skeggs 2004: 77–83). Skeggs gives an example which must be familiar to many, whether as a description of their own background, as naming a childhood lack, or as an expression of bourgeois acculturation:

> ... some activities, practices and dispositions can enhance the overall value of personhood: an example of which would be the cultural education of the middle class child who is taken to galleries, museums, ballet, music lessons, etc, activities which are all assumed to be morally 'good' for the person but which will also have an exchange value in later life as the cultural capital necessary for employability and social networking.
>
> (Skeggs 2004: 75)

As Skeggs argues, the dominant rhetoric of self-accumulation and its association with ideals of propriety means that those whose cultural location does not allow them to play this game are symbolically disadvantaged: 'a refusal to play the game or the lack of knowledge to participate in middle-class taste culture is read back onto the working class as an individualized moral fault, a problem of bad-choice, bad-culture, a failure to be enterprising or to be reflexive' (Skeggs 2004: 91).

Notwithstanding these difficulties with the distribution of the 'goods' of self-ownership, its rhetoric is extremely powerful and in many instances normatively attractive – in the context of law, it seems to add force to rights-claims, especially those felt to be fundamental, such as the right to liberty and autonomy. Paradoxically then, although law draws a (somewhat permeable) line between persons and property, insisting that persons are not property, nonetheless the extended metaphor of property seems to define and strengthen the notion of liberal selfhood (cf. Frow 1995; Davies and Naffine 2001: Chapter 1).

Such a view of the self may seem obvious and, moreover, it may seem ethically desirable. The concepts of self-possession and individual autonomy are said to secure our selves from interference by others, including the state, and define our liberty. They underline the limitedness and distinctiveness of being a human being. It is not hard to see that such representations of the person are not only abstractions but can have significant practical effects, right down to the level of control over one's body. Importantly, for those who have historically been regarded more as objects of property rather than self-owning subjects, the idea of self-ownership may provide a normative framework for asserting a right: for instance, pro-choice arguments are frequently cast in the language of self-ownership – a woman has the right to control her *own* body.

Before examining these debates in more detail, it is worth reiterating the constructedness of the individualistic, property-defined notion of the self. Such a notion may appear self-evident to those of us who are inculcated with the values of the liberal West. But it is by no means universal, as is evident by anthropological debates concerning a variety of different models of selfhood. Clifford Geertz, for instance, famously commented:

> The Western conception of the person as a bounded, unique, more or less integrated motivational and cognitive universe, a dynamic center of awareness, emotion, judgment, and action organised into a distinctive whole and set contrastively both against other such whole and against a social and natural

background is, however incorrigible it may seem to us, a rather peculiar idea within the world's cultures.

(Geertz, 1979: 229)

Without entering into the debate which Geertz's analysis provoked about a simplistic Western/non-Western dichotomy in the analysis of the self (Sökefeld 1999: 418; Murray 1993), and whether the Western self is truly 'peculiar' (Spiro 1993), it can fairly be stated that the understanding of the self varies between cultures. There may certainly be similarities and overlapping qualities in these different constructions of the self, and no clear dividing line between the many possible ideas of self. Yet there are discernable differences.

   To give just one of many possible examples, Deborah Bird Rose reports on a self-understanding of Indigenous Australians in the Victoria River District, Northern Territory:

It seems that subjectivity is not confined by the boundaries of the skin, but rather is sited both inside, on the surface of, and beyond the body. Subjects, then, are constructed both within and without: subjectivity is located within the site of the body, within the bodies of other people and other species, and within the world in trees, rockholes, on rock walls, and so on. And of course, location is by no means random; country is the matrix for the structured reproduction of subjectivities.

(Rose D. 1999: 180)

This self exists intrinsically in connection with what Westerners perceive as others – other people, other species, and the physical world. The isolated, self-contained and often competitive and materialistic individual, responsible essentially for his/her own existence, makes no sense in this context. Instead, responsibility is based in community connection and care, and not only of one's own blood relatives. Yet Rose warns against activists using Indigenous culture as a model for challenging Western paradigms: 'the problem for Westerners is to acknowledge the brokenness of our intersubjectivities, and to recuperate connection without fetishizing or appropriating Indigenous people and their culture of connection' (Rose D. 1999: 182).

   In quoting Rose on this point, I am of course pre-empting a crucial issue, that is, that the dominant Western notion of the self is problematic and needs to be rethought. Certainly there are many criticisms of the 'bounded self' as a paradigm of personality. Most straightforwardly, it has been criticised as an overstatement of one element of the tradition. While the notion of self-possession is certainly *present* in Western philosophical and political theory, there are other, more fluid and fragmentary notions of selfhood to be found in the philosophical literature (Murray 1993). Moreover, at the empirical level Westerners do not necessarily *experience* themselves in the way described by Geertz (Ewing 1990). Critical and post-modern theorists, meanwhile, have accepted that the bounded, autonomous individual is, in fact, the predominant model in Western philosophy. However, it is seen as a myth: subjects do not just exist as predetermined wholes with boundaries and essences, but find themselves in social networks, languages, discourses, and normative systems. We are intrinsically intersubjective beings, not single, separate entities (Lyotard 1984: 14–17).

From a socio-legal perspective, the main critical questions concern the broader cultural connotations of the notion of the bounded self and whether it is a useful normative construction.[4] The image of the person as self-proprietor, intrinsically divided as subject and object of property, is perceived by some to exacerbate, rather than ameliorate, the actual or potential commodification of persons. This is especially so when the 'goods' of self-ownership – like most property – are not evenly distributed. Symbolically, some positions in our social grammar are subjects while others are objects. Discursively, some *have* property, while others *are* property. I will come back to this later in the chapter, in relation to questions of sex, sexuality, and race, and will also return to these questions in Chapters 3 and 4.

The properties and property of law

Persons (ideal persons if not actual persons) are in this way often represented in legal and cultural discourse as bounded, as self-owners, and as independent units exclusive of other human entities. Exclusivity and the ability to exclude is of course a hallmark of a certain type of property. The notion that the person is bounded, discrete, and self-determining illustrates the metaphor of property in operation in relation to a fundamental aspect of human existence: our idea of our selves.

As a symbol of spatial containment and control, the proper also defines the terrains of positive law and of positivist jurisprudence as a discipline confined to understanding the positive law. John Austin insisted that the province of jurisprudence is determined, or we might say defined or delimited, by law 'properly so called':

> Laws proper, or properly so called, are commands; laws which are not commands, are laws improper or improperly so called.
>
> (Austin 1954: 1)

> And, since such is the principal purpose of the six ensuing lectures, I style them, considered as a whole, 'the province of jurisprudence determined.' For ... they affect to describe the boundary which severs the province of jurisprudence from the regions lying on its confines.
>
> (Austin 1954: 2)

Jurisprudence is a territory, and it has proper limits – those evident in the category of proper law, which is essentially positivist law. In the positivist tradition, law is only that which is named as law, which has the proper pedigree, the bloodline, the proper name of law. And moreover, to push the point a little further, the positivist concept of law has always co-existed rather uncomfortably with the common law: the common law is tolerated and comprehended by the proper positivist law. Yet precisely because it is common and not proper, of the people rather than born of a parliamentary naming process, it is not essential to law.

Thus when Jeremy Bentham said that 'property and law are born together and die together' (Bentham 1931: 113), I read this as more than an argument that property is only a creature of law, and not a natural right. There is a symbolic correspondence of law and property. There is sometimes a tendency to conflate any legal 'right' with property, and 'property' has sometimes been regarded as a kind of private sovereignty – property becoming a microcosm of law and the proprietor a mini-legislature (Cohen 1927; Vandevelde 1980: 328; Aoki 1996: 1311–15). Positive law itself is also conceptually based upon an originating exclusion, decision, or splitting which establishes a realm of law and a realm of that which is other to law. As Kelsen said of his pure theory:

> It characterises itself as a 'pure' theory of law, because it aims at cognition focused on the law alone, and because it aims to eliminate from this cognition everything not belonging to the object of cognition, precisely specified as the law. That is, the Pure

Theory aims to free legal science of all foreign elements. This is its basic methodological principle.

(Kelsen 1992: 7)

Interestingly, Kelsen does not say that his object 'law' is pure, merely that the theoretical cognition of law is pure or free of 'foreign elements' (Stewart 1998: 183; cf. Paulson 1992). Legal science takes an object of cognition – 'law' – and applies purely descriptive and analytical principles to the understanding of that object. Rather than beg the question of what is law and what is not, Kelsen's intention is to formulate necessary conceptual foundations for the cognition of law which are exclusive of material extraneous to law. However, as Peter Goodrich points out, the distinction between method and object may be illusory – '[h]ow we know an object is in large part constitutive of what that object is taken to be' (Goodrich 1983: 1; see also Svensson 2007). Legal philosophy, in other words, determines the contours of its object law as much as any self-contained law determines legal philosophy. Other theorists, with other methodologies, may construct a 'law' with different contours.

Austin and Kelsen might seem remote in some ways from contemporary legal thought, in particular as it relates to property. Nonetheless, they and other positivists have helped to determine the current predominant understanding of law. Of most significance is the idea that law has its own distinctive limits, and is separate from – and institutionally superior to – other normative orders. This limited law is, moreover, the proper domain of a pure jurisprudence or legal science: law and legal theory are co-extensive, both bound by the limited nature of law (Svensson 2007). In a sense, law is seen as present to jurisprudence – it is just there, self-identical and self-defining, a genuinely unified object, exclusive of unstable, disordered and otherwise unreliable social normativity.

At the practical level, the implications of the notion of 'proper law' are not difficult to discern. For instance, it seems incomprehensible to contemporary positivist-inspired law that a single physical space might be within the sphere of influence of several legal orders, unless these laws are strictly assimilated within the hierarchy of positive law. It is possible, of course, for elements of a religious or Indigenous legal order to be recognised and accommodated within the law, but any independent existence they have is foreclosed by the concept of the unitary and limited law. The order of proper positivist law is strictly monistic, not pluralistic. Law has one centre, one

identity, one sovereign. This account is, of course, increasingly challenged both by critical legal thought and by socio-legal approaches
which emphasise the pluralistic nature of law (Merry 1988; Melissaris
2004). Even less comprehensible than the co-existence of plural legal
regimes is that the physical place might have a law of its own, a
notion which is now often dismissed as unenlightened or supersti-
tious. The concept of 'the law of the land', meaning not the law
which belongs to a nation, but rather the law which emanates from
local places in manifold forms, is within the Western legal consciousness, but superseded by the positivist notion that all law emanates
from a singular human source and that localities are subordinated to
national political sovereignty.

The conflict in Australia over native title illustrates this last point
quite well. It is only when the relationship of Aboriginal people to
the land could be recast in terms comprehensible to Western law that
native title could be recognised. From the point of view of the parliament and judges the problem was how to render or reduce native
title into the single 'law' which governs Australia (Godden 2003;
Motha 2002). From other perspectives, such a process is nothing
more than continued appropriation in the name of a foreign law, and
may offer an insult to the law of the place, but obviously can do
nothing to override it. Irene Watson, for instance, comments that
'[n]ative title is the domain of those who want to establish space
rocket launching facilities and nuclear waste dumps; of those who
want it named and determined for their short time and space on
earth' (Watson 2002: 260). The proprietorial character of the positive law is therefore not only that it has the power to create and
recognise categories of property such as native title, but also that it in
a sense has complete and exclusive ownership over the territory
and the very question of law's identity – the horizon of positive
law thus understood therefore presumes a correspondence between
territory and jurisdiction, a singularity of sovereign possession, and
the total exclusion of any other potentially sovereign entity from the
terrain.

Proper knowledge

Within very specific parameters, certain ideational objects can formally, legally, be recognised as individual intellectual property: copy-
rights and patents give legal rights of excludability and use over ideas
taking a particular material form. On a more communal scale, areas

of vocational knowledge can be legally enclosed, giving professional collectives a monopoly over the practical use of a particular field of knowledge, such as installing electrical wiring in a house, auditing accounts, or performing neurosurgery. However, these instances of the legal regulation of knowledge are, like the legal recognition of self-ownership, only a limited symptom of a much broader cultural phenomenon. At a very abstract level, the cultural properties of knowledge are, like law, also inflected by the metaphor of the proper as that which is unified, coherent, distinct, autonomous, pure, self-identical. More concretely, knowledge is often analogised to real property, as a bounded terrain controlled by those designated experts in the field. Both the authority of expertise and the structure of positive objects of knowledge over which such authority is exercised can be seen as the effects of repeated acts of appropriation, exclusion, and boundary definition within discursive fields (cf. Foucault 1972; 1980: 68–9; Pottage 2004).

As I mentioned above, Derrida wrote of 'the metaphysics of the proper' – a metaphysics based on the 'reappropriation of difference' through values of propriety and the same. Such values include territorial limitation or separation of concepts determined with reference to notions of purity, essence, immediacy, singularity, individualism, self-possession, and presence (Derrida 1974: 26; see also Davies 1998). I have already indicated some of the ways in which this matrix of values influences perceptions of the self and the law. Derrida's point was, however, much broader because perceptions of the self and of law are merely sub-sets of cultural processes of representation: the language of the proper speaks through and structures thought generally and is therefore far more than an isolated symbol. Property as a defining characteristic, property as a thing which is our own, property as a right and as that which is right, and propriety in enacting our given social properties (such as our gender) are all interrelated concepts. In other words, what we know and the discourse we inhabit are strongly influenced by a metaphor and the metaphysics of the proper.

We can see this 'metaphysics of the proper' in common metaphors of knowledge and of academic disciplines as a sort of domain over which specialists have (often exclusive) mastery or control. As I indicated above, for instance, Austin determined the province of jurisprudence, the field of knowledge, as a kind of spatially limited territory, a form of real property (see also Davies M. 1996: 17–20; Douzinas et al. 1991: 25). Kant also analogised different forms of

knowledge, whether conceptual or empirical, to territories or physical domains (Kant 1952: 12). As Thomas Gieryn illustrates in relation to science, cartography is a widely used metaphor for the process
of delimiting specific fields of knowledge (Gieryn 1999: 6–12). But
the stakes are higher than merely charting the contours of an already-
existent terrain, since the spatial qualities of the field are inseparable
from the cultural distributions of credibility, epistemic authority and
ultimately power associated with mastery of an intellectual field.
Territorial metaphors were, for instance, frequently deployed reflex-
ively by Foucault to illustrate the relationship between knowledge
and power, and to suggest that the quality of that power is political
and juridical, not just geographical or natural:

> . . . let's take a look at these geographical metaphors. *Territory* is
> no doubt a geographical notion, but it's first of all a juridico-
> political one: the area controlled by a certain kind of power.
> *Field* is an economico-juridical notion. *Displacement*: what dis-
> places itself is an army, a squadron, a population. *Domain* is a
> juridico-political notion. *Soil* is a historico-geological notion.
> *Region* is a fiscal, administrative, military notion. *Horizon* is a
> pictorial, but also a strategic notion.
> . . . Once knowledge can be analysed in terms of region,
> domain, implantation, displacement, transposition, one is able
> to capture the process by which knowledge functions as a form
> of power and disseminates the effects of power. There is an
> administration of knowledge, a politics of knowledge, relations
> of power which pass via knowledge and which, if one tries to
> transcribe them, lead one to consider forms of domination
> designated by such notions as field, region and territory.
>
> (Foucault 1980: 68–9)

The spatial metaphors used by Foucault in his analysis of epistemic
territories are, in other words, not neutral and do not suggest that
knowledge occupies a naturally occurring space. Rather, they indicate that the distribution of knowledge/power is very much a matter
of control and excludability akin, if not entirely reducible, to legally
enforced distributions of land and other material commodities.

The notion that disciplines occupy or even metaphorically own
specific terrains of knowledge seems self-evident in the contemporary academic context, where we are accustomed to an ideational
carving-up of conceptual spaces and a corresponding allocation of

authority to those with an institutionally defined expertise in a field (Eden 2005: 283). While the broad disciplinary terrains (history, law, biological science) can appear fixed and even determined by their subject matter, sociologists of knowledge have, like Foucault, emphasised both the contingency of the disciplinary fields and the effort required to establish and maintain them. Thomas Gieryn, for instance, speaks of the 'credibility contests' and 'boundary work' which establish the terrain of scientific knowledge: '[t]he spaces in and around the edges of science are perpetually contested terrain; cultural maps are the interpretive means through which struggles for powerful ends are fought out – the right to declare a certain rendition of nature as "true" and "reliable" ' (Gieryn 1999: 15).[5] According to Gieryn, 'boundary work' takes the form of three different types of contest (1999: 15–18). First, 'expulsion' refers to the effort to determine which types of knowledge are 'legitimate' or inside the terrain of scientific knowledge: scientists must conform to specific conventions, and non-scientific pretenders are expelled. Second, 'expansion' takes place when 'two or more rival epistemic authorities square off for jurisdictional control over a contested ontological domain' (1999: 16). And third, 'protection of autonomy' names the efforts of those in control of a scientific terrain to ensure that their authority is not exploited by commercial or political interests, and that they retain the authority to self-determine (for an application to legal theory see Svensson 2007). The frontiers of disciplines are frequently naturalised, as though corresponding to an already-distinct object, but in fact these frontiers are the result of ongoing border disputes and claims of authority and control by scientists and other scholars. There is an inescapable proprietorial quality to these contests.

Fields of knowledge are, of course, constantly under pressure from adjacent or alternative fields. Indeed, in the contemporary academic climate, various forms of multi-, trans-, cross-, or interdisciplinary scholarship disrupt established categories, sometimes crystallising into new categories, with new boundaries and new experts, and sometimes remaining in a state of inter-territorial flux. In some instances, as Gieryn illustrates, this pressure occurs in an effort to establish or maintain an essential and proper domain of intellectual endeavour. In contrast, the more critical and reflexive sectors in the social sciences and humanities have attempted to destabilise fixed epistemic territories, either in a self-conscious attempt to resist the knowledge/power nexus, or simply in an effort to discover new fields and new methodologies by crossing the disciplinary divides. Judith Butler, for one, has argued against seeing feminism, lesbian/gay studies, or queer theory as 'proper objects' with fixed limits and distinctive intellectual hierarchies, suggesting that 'the time has come to encourage the kinds of conversations that resist the urge to stake territorial claims through the reduction or caricature of the positions from which they are differentiated' (Butler 1994: 21; see also Lattas 1989).

Legal theory has also become somewhat accustomed to transgressions across the territory of Austin's 'province of jurisprudence'. Legal theory is no longer seen as confined within the limits of a law defined narrowly by reference to hierarchically superior institutions or concepts. Both the object 'law' and methods for studying law cross fields as diverse as aesthetics, politics, economics, and social theory, among others. This is not to say that the study of law has lost its propriety, autonomy, or distinctiveness, but rather that critical theories of law have endeavoured to illustrate its reliance on discourses often constructed as 'other' to law.

BEYOND THE PROPER

So far, this chapter has sketched some of the resonances of property as a metaphor in the related discourses of knowledge, law and the person. I have tried to show, or at least suggest, some of the conceptual connections between these three ideational 'fields', as well as indicate the specific connotations of thinking about a particular object or field through the metaphor of property. Above all, the notions of exclusivity, boundedness, autonomy, immediate presence, and authority over the proper object (self, law, a field of knowledge), recur in the discussion. The property metaphor is one positive matrix for the construction of core Western values such as personal liberty and identity, the separation of law from politics and morality, and objective domains of knowledge. This is not to say that these values are *wholly* determined through the idea of the proper,[6] but that as a metaphor it somewhat influences and reinforces specific notions of self, law and knowledge.

The 'critical' dimension of the foregoing discussion lies in the attempt to elucidate something about the foundations of the Western liberal way of thinking. Unlike Kant's critiques, it does not attempt to posit the foundations of thought per se, but rather simply to identify and examine a particular cultural rhetoric which runs through several otherwise disparate fields. In the remainder of the chapter, and reflecting on the groundwork already laid out, two further senses of a critical approach to property will be considered. The first, a deconstructive approach, illustrates the ways in which the idea of property does not actually work in the way already discussed. This is an immanent or conceptually informed critique, because it looks at the presuppositions upon which the notion of 'the proper' is based. The second is a more socio-political critique, showing that the property metaphor has some other implications beyond those already discussed – that it is in fact a gendered metaphor in our cultural context, that it provides a language for the structuring of heterosexual relationships, and also that it has very strong racial overtones.

Deconstruction and the proper

The 'metaphysics of the proper' structures Western philosophy as well as aspects of the cultural imagination. In identifying and naming this phenomenon, Derrida laid open what he and others saw as the basic obsession of Western thought – its emphasis on sameness, similitude, identity, essences, rationality, and coherence in thought, rather than difference, discontinuity, gaps, and irrationality. Of course, in addition to the naming of the proper as a basis of Western thought, it became subject to Derrida's characteristic deconstructive approach, indicating how it is inevitably constituted by reference to its others, and how it cannot be a free-standing or pure concept, but is held in tension with other concepts. There is a formal or logical argument underlying the deconstruction of the proper, but it also has implications for the more 'applied' areas of philosophy which I have considered.

Derrida's formal argument deconstructing the proper is framed by reference to proper names, which are, in a sense, the archetype of the proper: the proper name is a direct, immediate reference, it ensures identity, and sets boundaries to a thing. The deconstruction of the proper name shows how this supposedly unique naming is in fact completely embedded in the common system of language.[7]

Let me explain this a little more carefully. (Out of propriety, politeness, and academic honesty, I should note that my interpretation takes place in the shadow of Geoffrey Bennington's thorough and subtle exposition: Bennington 1993: 104–14.) The proper name should involve direct, unique reference. It apparently attaches the name to the thing without having to justify itself in the web of differences and relationships which constitute common meaning. It just points at its object, or simply stands in for it. As Bennington says: 'Even if we accept that the system of langue is constituted by differences and therefore of traces, it would appear that the proper name, which is part of language, points directly toward the individual it names' (Bennington 1993: 104). As an instance of direct nomination, the proper name is not translatable, because it doesn't *mean* anything (Derrida 1985: 165–6; Derrida 1988: 100–4). To relate this to the discussion above, the proper person is self-contained and autonomous, proper law is distinct and different from social normativity at large, and proper fields of knowledge are bounded disciplines authorised by specific experts. Property itself, in one form, is seen primarily as a relationship between a unique 'I' and an object or thing.

However, the proper name is never entirely proper in its supposed singularity, because it has to be repeatable. For any name to do its work as a name, it cannot be an indivisible event: it must be *capable* of referring again and again, even if it is never uttered at all. Moreover, the repeatable is always *iterable* (Derrida 1977: 190): never unique, never itself, but always containing within the trace of the other against which it is continually defining itself. Bennington says it like this:

> . . . there is no proper name. What is called by the generic common noun 'proper name' must function, it too, in a system of differences: this or that proper name rather than another designates this or that individual rather than another and thus is marked by the trace of these others, in a classification . . . if only a two term classification.
>
> (Bennington 1993: 105)

In other words, and to simplify, the formal deconstructive argument is essentially that the proper must refer outside itself to that which is common, and to its (improper) other. It is never itself, and is therefore a non-identity, equally common and improper. To relate this thought to the concept of property, we could say that it is all very well to speak of a relationship between a person and a thing as the proper, distinct thing about property. However, its essence as *property* (in the sense accepted by Western legal thought) is to be found in the ability to exclude others. And what's more, the person–thing relationship has no meaning outside the couple 'I–it', unless and until it is acknowledged by law, that is, by a common set of meanings.

The formal argument also has its iterations in the extended cultural domain outlined in this chapter. As I mentioned earlier, for instance, late twentieth-century critiques of the subject moved away from the notion of the proper, bounded, self-determining individual towards a notion of inessential, intersubjective, contextualised beings.

Similarly, critiques of 'proper law' – in particular positivist theories of law – have emphasised the contingency and ideological nature of the notion of a limited (non-political, normatively separate) law. Clearly, there is a huge quantity of social law – we are overrun with conventions, norms, regulations, etiquette, proprieties, by-laws, stereotypes, patterns of thinking – but on what basis is there 'proper' law in Austin's sense, or 'pure' legal thought, in Kelsen's? As soon as we try to identify a law which is separate and self-referential, it evaporates into nothingness, or resolves into something which it is not – such as a fiction (Kelsen 1991), the command of a sovereign (Austin 1954), recognition by officials (Hart 1994). Perhaps the law can only reside in an act of force which creates and preserves its identity as 'proper' or separate (Derrida 1991). In other words, an ongoing ideological *act* sustains the concept of law as proper even though we know that law, like the proper name, subsists only within social, linguistic, economic, and political systems of significance. (As I explained above, a similar though sociologically based argument was made by Gieryn about the domains of knowledge: they do not exist naturally but are maintained by 'credibility contests' and 'boundary work'.) Thus one of the things which postmodernism brings to the contemporary analysis of law is an understanding that the idea of law cannot be what its positivist proponents have claimed, even though the practice and much of the theory of law may still operate on the assumption that this idea is real and practicable. Instead of hierarchy, singularity and exclusion, a non-proprietorial understanding of law emphasises the horizontal, plural, social spaces of law, for instance as a network rather than a pyramid (Ost and Van de Kerchove 2002). (Or equally this may be a 'proprietorial' form of law, but one which sees property as relational, contextual, and dynamic.)

As I have implied, the breakdown of the opposition between proper and common can also be seen in twentieth-century commentary on the nature of property, in particular by post-Hohfeldian anguish over the loss of the proper in property. As I explained in Chapter 1, the cornerstone of Hohfeld's analysis of property was the notion that rights *in rem* (against the world) are in essence a multitude of rights *in personam* (against a person) (1917). The proper, distinct nature of property and in particular the direct, present, immediate, singular relationship between me and mine thus became common, intersubjective, and indirect (Edgeworth 1988; Grey 1980). Recent attempts to reappropriate property, rescuing it from the clutches of its improper others (such as contract, which is essentially inter-personal) respond to a need to have things in their proper, correct, individuated, place (Penner 1997: 1–2).

Having and being

These immanent types of critique look at the logical foundations of the concepts of proper persons, law, and knowledge. There are also more socially grounded criticisms which consider the cultural and political connotations of the metaphor of property. In this and the next section, I will outline some of the criticisms of the notion of the self-possessed person which have been made by feminists and race scholars. These critiques do not question the metaphor of property on merely conceptual grounds (though that critique is sometimes presupposed), but by reference to the way that it works in social, political and legal discourse.

As indicated above, the 'possessive individual' depicted the white, middle-class male who epitomised early liberal values of autonomy and self-accumulation. Contemporary critics have argued that these characteristics of whiteness, masculinity and class status continue to inflect the notion of self-possession as a cultural and political value, despite the formal legal extension of equal rights to all. The archetype of the possessive individual remains a white, middle-class male, while 'others' are regarded as objects or lacking the cultural capital which makes a person. Beverley Skeggs, for instance, has argued that the cultural property of Western selves is associated with middle class, accumulative modes of self-production (2004).

Some groups have historically been regarded as owned objects and have therefore struggled to attain the self-possession necessary for personhood. Cheryl Harris has analysed the historical and contemporary resonances of whiteness as a form of self-owned and self-defining property (Harris 1993). Historically in the US, whiteness was a valuable property for several related reasons: as slaves Black people were literally objects of property, and could not themselves be proprietors[8]; whiteness was accorded status, privileges, rights, and immense value; and the borderline between whiteness and blackness was policed rigorously. Whiteness was an exclusive territory, unavailable to African Americans, and characterised by its legal, moral, and racial purity.[9] Harris says 'whiteness and property share a common premise – a conceptual nucleus – of a right to exclude' (Harris 1993: 1714; see also Bell 1995). And in relation to the legal delineation of whiteness – 'In effect, the courts erected legal "No Trespassing" signs' (Harris 1993: 1741). The metaphors of purity, boundary, and territorial exclusion are thus evidenced in the legal concept of whiteness which underpinned much of the history of race relations in the United States. Harris goes further than this, however, and argues that property in whiteness is still very much a part of the context of law, most obviously because whiteness has an undisputed value in the social marketplace and because of the 'othering' and exclusion of non-white identities through legal and other mechanisms.

The racialisation of the property-person nexus – representations of whiteness as a valuable property of self-possessed persons and of non-white human beings more directly as objects of property or economic instruments – is not confined to the legacy of legal slavery. Colonialism in Australia was (and still is) premised on the appropriation of space, power and culture by people who regarded themselves intrinsically as owners from people who the colonialists generally regarded as non-owners (Moreton-Robinson 2005a; 2005b; cf. Coombe 1993). 'Ownership' in this context means a particular form of control and use of a resource for economic purposes, not a sustainable custodianship of the physical environment (Watson 1997). In Canada, the United States and New Zealand the making of treaties or settlements with Indigenous peoples indicates some level of acknowledgement of Indigenous ownership and/or territorially based sovereignty: this did not prevent the colonial histories of these nations being characterised by forceful dispossession, initially through the mapping and proper naming of the colonies (Dorsett and McVeigh 2002: 299–300) and subsequently through a variety of technologies of appropriation (see, for example, Kelsey 1995). I will come back to the relationship of culture, colonialism and property in each of the next three chapters.

The heterosexual economy

Unlike male and female slaves, white women were never regarded legally as property which could be bought, sold, and destroyed at will. However, a strong cultural association of masculinity with self-ownership and femininity with object-property status has persisted in spite of liberal claims of equality. Until the twentieth century this was reinforced by the legal disabilities of married women: while the married woman was not technically property, nor was she an independent legal person, and could own little property herself.

Both Ngaire Naffine and Jennifer Nedelsky have emphasised the ways in which the image of the self-owning person is a social image of masculinity. For Nedelsky legal persons are defined ideologically through the metaphor of private property as a kind of territory with rigid boundaries, reinforced by the notion of individual rights, which strengthen the separation between the person and the State, and between the private domain and the public sphere: 'the image of protective boundaries as essential to the integrity and autonomy of the self is deep and pervasive in our culture' (Nedelsky 1990: 168). This legal 'bounded self' is not only a trope for abstract autonomy, but as Naffine illustrates in relation to the criminal law, it is also a literal quality of our bodies: 'The person presupposed by the law of assault is a discrete, distinct, volitional subject for whom the skin of his body is considered to represent a boundary from other distinct subjects' (Naffine 1997: 85). Such an image of the self may appear to be available to both women and men. However, as both Nedelsky and Naffine argue, it is a metaphor of the self which is normatively masculine. Women are more likely to be seen as normatively *unbounded*: as relational selves, carers, and physically penetrable (Nedelsky 1990: 170). In social depictions of heterosexual sex, women are traditionally the ones who surrender their boundaries: according to Naffine this view of sex is also represented in law. Thus, women have to continually reassert the argument for the protection of their bodily integrity, rather than have it taken for granted.

Such imagery indicates that the property–person relationship is thoroughly gendered, though it should be noted that this gendering relies upon specific and constructed conceptions of property, masculinity, and female identity. Because property is typically seen in territorial, closed, and inviolable terms, conceptions of self-ownership more closely reflect social constructions of the male body, rather than the female body, which is supposedly lacking such clear frontiers. The operative concept of property in this context is property as private sovereignty.

A further cause of feminist concern over the property–person relationship is that it seems to commodify persons, and that this is expressed most strongly in the commodification of women and sexuality. Self-ownership requires a division between the self as a subject and the self as a physical or ideational object. Since women are not traditionally represented as subjects in language, law, philosophy, or in the symbolic order generally, 'self'-ownership is not an automatic social entitlement for women. Rather, object status has often been the cultural default position (MacKinnon 1982: 515; Irigaray 1985: 170–97) and heterosexual relationships have all too frequently been understood as relationships of ownership and exchange of women (Pateman 1988). In its construction of domestic relationships, the common law also reinforced the view that women were the property of their husbands (Conaghan 1998: 137–8).

The perception that the property–person nexus is gendered has prompted several quite different types of response. First, Nedelsky argues that the boundary metaphor produces an impoverished and politically inappropriate notion of the person. It should be rethought in favour of an intersubjective, connected conception of the person which would not draw on gender stereotypes (Nedelsky 1990). Such a rethinking would address both the gendered nature of property–person symbolism, *and* the fact that the bounded individual is arguably not the most positive model for legal personhood. Many feminists have argued that connection and relationality are more productive human values than separation and individualism, and that such values ought to be reflected in legal norms.

Second, from a pragmatic point of view, and recognising the pervasiveness of the commodity culture, Radin argues that ownership, including self-ownership, does in fact help to define and protect a person's autonomy. However, the core attributes of the person should be regarded as 'market inalienable' for women and men alike (Radin 1987). After all, the non-discrimination rhetoric of liberalism works very effectively when it is required to extend a limited class of person to a more inclusive class of person: if no rational ground can be found for distinguishing between exclusive and inclusive concepts of person in a particular context, liberalism has tended over time to favour the more inclusive concept. The history of the suffrage illustrates this point extremely well. Thus, it can be argued that the rhetoric of self-ownership protects the person, and that women should make the most of this rhetoric in order to protect their personal and bodily autonomy. As Nedelsky frankly points out, 'property looks to some like the perfect vehicle to power and autonomy and to others like the path to oppression' (Nedelsky 1993: 350).

A third approach accepts the rhetorical power of self-ownership, but argues that the operative concept of ownership ought to be reformulated. As Rosalind Petchesky argues, 'to reject that language [of self-ownership] wholesale is to leave those without property nothing at all to own' (Petchesky 1995: 400). Davina Cooper suggests a similar line of argument in her discussion of the two senses of 'belonging' (Cooper 2007: 629). In the first – the hierarchical 'subject–object' sense, the thing which belongs to me is separate from me, and I have mastery over it. In the second, belonging is 'a relationship of connection, of part to whole' (ibid): in this sense, I belong to a family, or an artistic style belongs to a specific cultural group. Such a notion of belonging engenders a quite different idea of property in which connection is central, and there is a 'constitutive' and non-separable relationship between the terms of the relationship. Thinking of ownership in a relational and caretaking sense may alleviate the gendered dimensions of self-ownership rhetoric, because rather than imply self-mastery, it connotes connection with and obligation to the self and others. Thus, rather than rejecting the property–person relationship altogether or accepting the paradigm but trying to ensure it becomes an inclusive model, the suggestion is that property in the self and at large be redefined in some of the terms offered by contemporary critical and feminist thought. I will come back to the question of redefining property at the end of Chapter 4, and in Chapter 5.

CONCLUSION

This chapter has dealt with the symbolism of property in several cultural spheres. It would have been possible to write at much greater length and in far greater detail. I have not even touched on a number of significant issues – for instance the informal deployment of property rhetoric in carving up and appropriating social and political spaces (Moran and Skeggs 2001), the propriety of dividing the world into subjects and objects (see Davies 1999), or the whole socio-legal and anthropological issue of commodification – how things come to be regarded as commodities and what the social impact of this is (Ertman and Williams 2005). Nonetheless, I hope to have done enough here to illustrate some of the extended meanings of property, and how the 'thought of the proper' inflects the Western, and in particular the liberal Anglo-American, cultural consciousness. Many of the themes I have raised here will reappear in later chapters.

Notes

1　This opening thought presumes a particular experience of the mind–body connection. On the other hand, as Davina Cooper has pointed out to me, the example of conjoined twins indicates that this is not a universal experience.
2　By 'extra-legal' I refer to practices not formally accepted by positive law. For instance, one extra-legal way in which the dualism of person and property is circumvented is by the illegal trafficking in persons. Another, which is non-legal rather than illegal, is by the cultural representation of women and children as commodities.
3　Depending on one's interpretation, for instance, it could be said that genetic information derived from a person can be owned by another (Boyle 1992: 1508–19), or that – in certain jurisdictions – the use of a person's image for commercial purposes is their property (Dangelo 1989). Moreover, it might be argued that even while law excludes property in the person, some legal doctrines or business practices can have property-like effects on persons – for instance when a person's own right over their body is removed for some reason or where sporting stars are 'bought' and 'sold' in a transfer market. See generally Davies and Naffine 2001; Calabresi 1991.
4　Other core issues concern the extent to which the bounded self is actually reflected in law and whether the legal view of the person is in transition, though I do not propose to address these matters here.
5　I am indebted to Eva-Maria Svensson for first bringing Gieryn's work to my attention. See Svensson 2007.
6　Derrida suggests that the 'metaphysics of the proper' – involving the thoughts of sameness and difference, conceptual containment, authority, logocentrism, the subject–object distinction – does in fact inform Western philosophy on a general scale. I agree with him as far as the primary structure of language/discourse/thought is concerned, but because my analysis is more about the secondary uses of property as socio-cultural metaphor, I would stop short of making such a broad claim.
7　The following four paragraphs are an abridged and revised version of Davies 1998: 170–72.
8　A fact ironically referred to in the title of Patricia Williams' well-known article 'On Being the Object of Property' and in various chapters in Harriet Beecher Stowe's novel *Uncle Tom's Cabin*, for instance Chapter 5, 'Showing the Feelings of Living Property on Changing Owners' and Chapter 11, 'In Which Property Gets into an Improper State of Mind'.
9　As Harris explains, although some persons with more than a drop of Black blood could be considered white, the legal definitions of Blackness were designed to ensure a strict delimitation of a territory of whiteness into which no one could cross who did not satisfy the blood requirements laid down by law.

Chapter 3

Histories

> Our language can be seen as an ancient city: a maze of little streets and squares, of old and new houses and of houses with additions from various periods; and this surrounded by a multitude of new boroughs with straight regular streets and uniform houses.
>
> (Wittgenstein 1958: §18)

HOW? WHO? WHAT?

In Chapter 2 I outlined aspects of the cultural symbolism of property which operate in the various social spheres of the contemporary liberal West: spheres such as law, politics, identity-formation, and sexual identity. As I explained, property and its associated concepts of propriety and the proper are immensely powerful normative symbols for a way of life. In contrast, this and the next chapter present more conventional dimensions of the property-concept, that is, its history and theory. These three issues – meanings, history, and theory – can be seen as three sides of a triangular cultural matrix of property: each in a sense has its own sphere and its own logic, but each element is constitutive of and dependent upon the others. For instance, it is possible to isolate property as a symbol or metaphor for a variety of human interactions. But as I hope to show in this chapter, it is ultimately impossible to disentangle this symbolism from historical developments such as feudalism, colonialism, the abolition of slavery and the married women's property enactments. In the next chapter, which outlines the more abstract side of property, it will also become evident that history and symbolism co-exist with some rather momentous theoretical interventions such as Locke's 'labour' justification of property which both named and strengthened the logic of colonial expansion (Locke 1988: 285–6).

Two introductory points about history are significant. First, although I speak sometimes of the 'development' of the idea of property, this should not be understood as a linear evolution of a single idea with its own coherence and continuity. Rather, I see the history of property as a coming together of a large number of diverse and sometimes antagonistic historical influences – ideas, social movements, economic and political imperatives, events – which have contributed to a complex, layered, and pluralistic concept with extensive legal and cultural resonance (cf. Foucault 1972: 21–30). There is no intrinsic logic to the development of property. This does not entail a total rejection of Marx's notion of a historical material-ist dialectic in which economic relations (including actual owner-ship distributions) determine a superstructural ideology of property ownership, among other things (Marx 1859: 181). However, in keep-ing with twentieth-century interpretations of Marxist thought, it does suggest that the logic of economic conditions alone cannot fully explain the complexity of a pluralistic concept like property (cf. Althusser 1994; Jameson 1994). The pluralistic potential of property will be outlined in more detail in Chapter 5.

Second, thinking of property as a historical and cultural artefact accepts that what we in liberal common-law countries know as 'property' is not universal, but is rather a product of a specific con-text. Nor is our concept of property the end point of an evolution-ary process tending towards an ideal. It is just the here-and-now of a cultural and political history which is still in process. This is not to say that contemporary liberal property has nothing in common with other, non-Western, regimes for allocating the use and control of resources, but rather that its grammar, its constructions of subject and object, its notion of boundaries and control, combine in a dis-tinctive and layered form. Certainly the liberal Western understand-ing of property is a dynamic form which is particularly influential throughout the world, increasingly so as a result of global capital-ism, but it is not the only possible method of understanding the relationship between person and thing, or between persons in rela-tion to things. Having said that, this is not a comparative book. While it is important to be aware of other understandings of the person–thing nexus, an analysis of these forms is not my purpose (but see generally Hann 1998; Pottage and Mundy 2004).

Instead, I want to draw out three dimensions of the history of property, that is the historical variations of how ownership is organised legally, who can own, and what can be owned. Or, How? Who? and What? Like everything in this book, these angles are linked – for instance, as far as who and what are concerned, one aspect of the relationship is that the individual human being is now normally seen as the archetypal owner *as well as* the archetypal entity which *cannot* be owned. A person can own, but not be, property. (As I have indicated in Chapter 2, the situation is in reality far more complex than this, given the liberal rhetoric of *self*-ownership.) This was not always the case. Until the nineteenth century many Western legal systems permitted human beings to be the objects of property. And, in some contexts, there was more emphasis upon communal, rather than individual, ownership. Thus there have been large shifts in the How, Who, and What of property. It is not possible to analyse these shifts comprehensively so, within each heading, I have chosen one or two themes which elaborate on those initially raised in Chapter 1.

HOW? PROPERTY AND POWER

There are many dimensions to any discussion of the fundamental nature of property, or how it is organised legally. As I indicated in Chapter 1, a persistent question is whether property has a core or essential meaning, or whether it is just a bundle of indicative rights, some of which must be present in order for a person–thing nexus to be characterised as proprietorial. The 'bundle of rights' picture is more prevalent as a legal characterisation of property, even though the popular cultural and symbolic view of property casts it as rather solid and tangible. Another matter, which is my main focus in this part of the chapter, concerns the socio-political significance of property and, in particular, the extent to which property-ownership has had a formal relationship with the owner's status as citizen, family member, or political agent.

Private property undoubtedly confers certain forms of power on owners, modulated in part by the variations in who can own, what they can own, and how they own it. In terms of 'who', for instance, the common law rule that a woman's property passed to her husband upon marriage gave men direct power over their wives. Or, in relation to 'what', the term of a patent – for instance in a pharmaceutical invention – gives the patent-holder power to control access to medical treatment. *Intrinsic* to the existence of private property is the power to control the object, whatever it is, and the power to exclude others from its use and enjoyment. Property is essentially a power relation (Gray 1991). More specifically, it is 'an abbreviated reference to a quantum of socially permissible power exercised in respect of socially valued resources' (Gray and Gray 1999: 12).

Power over things and over people is therefore essential to the legal notion of property. However, the power of property extends far beyond its formal incidents. There are obviously many coincidental forms of social and political power which accrue to people who own: most importantly in the liberal context property brings choices which cannot be so freely exercised by the non-propertied – the choice of where to live and how; the choice of type and level of education; the means of litigating your rights (or attempting to squash another's rights) in a court of law should you choose to; or the means of having your opinions heard in the corridors of political power. Clearly, private property is one important factor in the *actual* distribution of forms of personal, political, economic, social, or legal power.

At this point the property–power nexus becomes a complex socio-political phenomenon. On the one hand, the core contemporary liberal concept of private property insists that the power associated with it is essentially (formally) of a private and individual nature, and does not affect a person's legal status, their legal right to participate politically, or their legal influence over their family. Property ownership is seen as a shield for the individual against the state and against other individuals (Reich 1991). It is also seen as a means of enhancing individual liberty (Radin 1987), but it does not formally entail that the owner has greater rights (except in relation to her property) than anyone else. At least, that is the myth by which property and its unequal distribution is said to be consistent with the equality of all human beings (see Cotterrell 1987: 82).

On the other hand, this liberal picture of property, with its individualising discourse and its focus upon formal rights, does little to come to terms with the structural, ideological, and symbolic dimensions of property–power. It is a depoliticising cover story, which relegates the status of property to a private arrangement endorsed and enforced by the state, but otherwise only incidentally connected to political power (see generally Blomley 2004: 4–7). The liberal narrative is an immensely powerful, but ultimately unconvincing, myth: after all, who really believes that everyone, regardless of their financial worth, their social properties, or their racial capital,[1] can (even now in the twenty-first century) participate equally in the political processes of the state, let alone the quasi-public spheres of media, education, and commerce?

Property was not always formally separated from power over other people in Western history, and in some instances this separation is relatively recent. In some cases, as Drahos and Braithwaite have argued in relation to intellectual property, ownership increasingly consists of both a right to exclude others *and* a right to dictate to others, thus compromising the separation of property from power (Drahos and Braithwaite 2002). First of all, then, some exploration of the relationship between property and various forms of familial, personal and political power is warranted: this contributes to an understanding of the actual and formal relationship of power to the concept of property.

Familial power

> If a father sell his son three times, the son shall be free from his father.
>
> (Twelve Tables IV.2)

One interesting angle on this question takes us back to the earliest expressions of property–power in Roman law. Roman law is well known as the origin of *dominium* or 'Roman ownership of a Roman thing acquired by a Roman process' (Thomas 1976: 133). The concept of *dominium* changed throughout the approximately 1,000 years of Roman legal development, but at its core *dominium* was limited to a Roman 'who', 'what' and 'how'. It was (and still is) known as a nearly absolute and indivisible type of ownership, in contrast to the more relative and divisible forms of common law property (Gray and Symes 1981: 21).

Dominium seems to have crystallised from a more generalised concept of power. In the earliest times patriarchal power named the control of the male head over his household, which included wife, children, slaves, animals, land, and chattels. It was essentially the power of the household head over all the contributing elements of a rural economy and included, for instance, the power of life and death over children and the power to sell them. Gradually the forms of power were differentiated by the object of the power and its economic significance, as explained by Maine:

> Patriarchal Power of all sorts appears ... to have been once
> conceived as identical in character, and it was doubtless dis-
> tinguished by one name. The Power exercised by the ancestor
> was the same whether it was exercised over the family or the
> material property – over flocks, herds, slaves, children, or wife.
> ... But, when Roman law has advanced a little, both the name
> and the idea have become specialized. Power is discriminated,
> both in word and in conception, according to the object over
> which it is exerted. Exercised over material commodities or
> slaves, it has become *dominium* – over children, it is *Potestas* –
> over free persons whose services have been made away to
> another by their own ancestor, it is *mancipium* – over a wife, it is
> still *manus*.
>
> (Maine 1920: 330–31)

On this account, *dominium* and the other forms of power over persons and things was distilled from the general power of the household head. *Dominium* is just one expression of a broad patriarchal
power. Diósdi hypothesises that the reasons for the differentiation in
forms of power were political and economic. Primarily, the Roman
Empire expanded greatly during the third and second centuries BC
resulting in a large influx of slaves (who were the spoils of war). The
larger number of slaves meant that they were no longer seen personally as members of a household, while the economic value of other
members of the household (that is, family) declined. A legal difference therefore evolved between persons who were simply owned as
fungible objects together with other 'things', and those 'free' persons
who were nonetheless under the control of a personal form of power
(Diósdi 1970: 132).

Patriarchal power with some of these property-like characteristics
of control and exclusion was also a feature of the common law. Until
the late nineteenth century, married women could not own property
independently since, under the doctrine of coverture, the wife's legal
personality was 'incorporated and consolidated' into the person of
her husband (Blackstone 1765: 430). She had no independent legal
status and therefore no ability to own property, enter into contracts
or bring litigation under the common law. Her prior personal property was owned outright by the husband, while he also had the right
to possession and profits in relation to any real property (Baker 1990:
552). This incapacity to own could be circumvented in some ways
by the law of equity which recognised a distinction between a legal

owner and the beneficiary of a trust: the legal title to a woman's property might be held by someone other than her husband, on trust for her (see generally Stretton 1998: 25–9; Perkin 1989: 15–19), thus separating her property from that of her husband. Needless to say, such arrangements mainly benefited relatively wealthy women.

While coverture did not make the woman into a chattel (such as a slave, who could be bought and sold on an open market), it is certainly not an overstatement to say that the husband–wife relationship displayed many of the incidents of a property relationship in which wives took the part of the object: the wife had no independent legal personality, reduced capacity to own property herself, and her husband was legally permitted to physically abuse her. (For instance, a wife could be lawfully subjected to limited physical violence and could not effectively withhold consent to sexual intercourse: amazingly this 'marital rape exemption' lasted almost until the twenty-first century in many common law countries which had otherwise accepted gender equality.[2]) The law of torts compensated various injuries to men on the basis that 'a wife's person was her husband's property' (Conaghan 1998: 138).

> Thus, a husband could seek damages from another for enticing his wife to leave him or harbouring her without lawful justification; a male adulterer could be sued by a wronged husband under an action known as 'criminal conversation'; and in an action *per quod consortium amisit* or *servitium amisit* a husband had a right to sue another if, by virtue of a tort committed against his wife, he was deprived of her society and/or services.
>
> (Conaghan 1998: 137–8)

Although married women were not regarded as alienable property in the common law,[3] there was nonetheless a strong undercurrent of property-related principles which commodified both married and unmarried women under cover of the family and the private sphere. These legal forms were, of course, supplemented by and interwoven with far-reaching (and ongoing) cultural narratives, which imagine the woman as sexual object, fungible economic resource, or the means of (re)producing heirs and labour (Naffine 1998; Davies 1994; McCoin 1998; Schroeder 1994b).

Children have also been regarded as more like property than persons, their identity also concealed by the notion of the (male-headed) family. They were subject to the *patria potestas* of Roman law. This condition did not naturally lapse upon the child reaching maturity, but instead endured for the life of the father: sons were only released from it by the death of all direct paternal ancestors (or, as the *Twelve Tables* says, by being sold three times), while women generally remained in the power of a male for their entire life (Watkin 1999: 166–8; Johnston 1999: 30–33).

Children were not technically or legally *owned* under the common law, but were nonetheless almost entirely governed by paternal power (cf. Conaghan 1998: 138). Until the twentieth century, the child was an economic resource whose exploitation was more or less accepted (Freeman 1983: 13–16). Some writers argued that paternal power constituted ownership: Robert Filmer, for example, the author of the (monarchist and anti-liberal) seventeenth-century political treatise *Patriarcha*, argued that people are not born free, but are under the direct subjection of their father:

> Every man that is born, is so far from being free-born, that by his very birth he becomes a subject to him that begets him: under which subjection he is always to live, unless by immediate appointment from God, or by the grant or death of his Father, he becomes possessed of that power to which he was subject.
>
> (Filmer 1949: 232)[4]

Children were very much property within this view:

> God also hath given to the Father a right or liberty to alien[ate] his power over his children, to any other; whence we find the sale and gift of children, to have been much in use in the beginning of the world.
>
> (Filmer 1949: 231)

Filmer's views about patriarchal power, its use as the foundation of all political power, as well as his dubious Biblical deductions, were challenged in John Locke's *First Treatise of Government*. In relation to the specific notion that begetting a child (or labouring to create it) justified power over her or him, Locke pointed out that according to Christian thought, God, rather than individual fathers, was actually the author and originator of all people (Locke 1967: 178–9). Moreover, if contribution to a child's existence is seen as justification for power over them, then 'no body can deny but that the Woman hath an equal share, if not the greater' (Locke 1967: 180; see generally

Archard 1993). (This is not to say that Locke's philosophy promoted equality, as we will see in Chapter 4.)

As is the case with women, however, the philosophical rejection of the notion that children can be owned as chattels did not erase this notion from the cultural or indeed the legal imagination. While the common law did not go as far as the Roman law in allowing outright selling of children into slavery, children have certainly been regarded more as objects of others' rights, rather than subjects of rights, and therefore more like property than person (Hart 1991; Freeman 1983: 13–19). While the days have ended (at least in most parts of the world) where parents can transfer their rights over children by a contract of indentured servitude, rights are nonetheless exercised by other persons or entities who, in the contemporary world, are supposed to put the child's interest first. But that does not secure the subjectivity of the child. Michael Freeman, for instance, made the point only 20 years ago that the personhood of children is compromised by legal rules which still distribute power over the child between parents, doctors, teachers, guardians, the state, and so forth: 'The object (I would like to call her or him a person but this is hardly permissible) is curiously dehumanised to the point of becoming a piece of land over which there is a boundary dispute' (Freeman 1983: 160). Thus, despite the explicit legal position that children are not objects of property, the power of social rhetoric – especially that connected with parental rights – is such that the subjectivity of the child is all too easily erased.

Imperial power: land, lord and locality

Roman law also distinguished between *imperium*, the public power held by a sovereign or state, and *dominium*, the private power of individual ownership (cf. Cohen 1927). In countries which have inherited some version of Roman law, this distinction is reflected in strongly separated spheres of public and private law. As I have already indicated, contemporary liberal legal thought also attempts a formal (if not substantive) separation between power exercised in the public political realm and the merely private power of ownership. Again, such a distinction has not always been a feature of the common law. Indeed, the feudal society out of which the common law arose was characterised by the lack of a clear distinction between political and personal power (Samuel 1999: 40–45). This was not due, as in Roman society, to a tightly controlled familial structure but rather to the manner in which all people were effectively tied to land, lord and locality. As Vinogradoff put it: 'The status of a person depended in every way on his position on the land, and on the other hand, land-tenure determined political rights and duties' (Vinogradoff 1957: 458).

At first, as in the Roman state, property did not have a distinct nature: rather, it grew out of a changing legal and social order. In England, after the Norman Conquest, all landholders, except the monarch, were tenants in a hierarchy of subinfeudated land (Simpson, 1986: 5). No one had 'owned' land in the contemporary sense, since any landholding was normally conditional upon the performance of a service: major landholders would supply soldiers in times of need, religious organisations might say mass for the lord, and villeins would undertake agricultural service (Simpson 1986: 7–15). In an essentially agricultural society, most people had some formal tie to a plot of land. In addition, land could not be alienated without the consent of the lord, it could not be devised by will, and it would revert to the lord in certain circumstances such as where a landholder died without an heir. The lack of freedom in relation to land holding and the reciprocal obligations bound up with land leads Baker to comment that '[f]eudal tenure was the antithesis of ownership as we know it' (Baker 1990: 262; see also Atiyah 1979: 86).

This conditional landholding gave rise to a situation in which public status and control over others was directly related to a person's estate, or their formal position in the landholding hierarchy. Over a period of some centuries accumulated practical and technical legal changes meant that landholders gradually became freed from most of the incidents of tenure while land became more easily alienable and more like property. However, the feudal association of public power with landholding and its associated status categories has taken centuries of both legal reform and liberal rhetoric to overcome. Even where the more explicit feudal connection of landholding with power became fractured, it was succeeded, as Carol Rose argues, by a more subtle and more pervasive assumption that public order and 'propriety' were indissoluble with property. Rose cites the corporate colonial enterprises such as the East India Company where 'the proprietors and charter holders acquired not only monopolistic property rights in their respective colonial enterprises but also the right and duty to govern the colonial charges and keep them in proper order' (Rose 1994: 60).

A simple illustration of the formal association of property with public power relates to suffrage and the ability to sit as a member of parliament. In early 'democratic' processes, it was common for voting rights to be granted only to men who held a certain amount of property. In Britain, for instance, the Great Reform Act of 1832 essentially granted the vote to adult males who held land worth £10 (or a greater or lesser value in certain cases: see generally Phillips and Wetherell 1995). This was followed in 1867 by a further Reform Act which granted suffrage to all male householders including, for the first time, working-class men. In South Australia (where this book is being written) suffrage was granted to all adult men for the first election for the lower house of parliament in 1857, while the upper house retained the British tradition of being formed as a 'house of property' meaning that suffrage, and the ability to be elected, was restricted to adult men with a 'freehold estate in possession' to the value of £50 or a leasehold with at least three years to run to the value of £25 per annum (Jaensch 2002: 32). The property restrictions were progressively relaxed throughout the twentieth century but amazingly were not completely abolished until 1973 (Jaensch 2002: 30–36).

Even more interesting is the recent history of House of Lords reform in Britain. Hundreds of hereditary peers sat in the upper house of parliament until the House of Lords Act of 1999: elevated personal status or title was itself a form of property which at the highest level automatically brought with it political standing in parliament. From time to time such titles were openly purchased from the monarch or his/her delegates (Stone 1958; Mayes 1957).[5] The reform of 1999 eliminated the automatic right of hereditary peers to sit in parliament but, ironically, left them represented by 92 peers *elected* by their number. (That is, as one newspaper columnist put it, creating the 'absurd paradox' that the 'only elected members [in the House of Lords] are people born to the job . . . chosen by means of an ermine-clad election in 1999, in which franchise was granted by birthright'.[6]) As a remnant of the feudal association of property with political standing, the hereditary peerage and the House of Lords are even now proving resistant to modernisation (McLean et al. 2003).[7]

The feudal relationship of landed property and personal status with political power has therefore left symbolic traces in the notion of 'property as propriety' as well as formal traces in contemporary (though nearly extinct) notions of hereditable political rights. More insidiously, as I have indicated, private property gives rise to actual, if not legally entrenched, public power. The feudal ability of lords to dictate to their vassals is also arguably being reinvented in a sphere remote from medieval distributions of land: that of intellectual property. That at least is the argument compellingly proposed by Peter Drahos and John Braithwaite in *Information Feudalism* (2002). In their account, protection of intellectual property which is not counterbalanced by the interests of the community generally can lead to 'information cartels' with an unjustifiable level of power over information resources:

> In the case of medieval feudalism, the relationship of the lord to the land and vassals was a relationship of great inequality. The majority of humble folk were subject to the private power that lords exercised by virtue of their ownership of the land. This private power became, in effect, governmental power as lords set up private manorial systems of taxes, courts and prisons. The redistribution of property rights in the case of information feudalism involves a transfer of knowledge assets from the intellectual commons into private hands. These hands belong to media conglomerates and integrated life sciences corporations rather than individual scientists and authors. The effect of this, we argue, is to raise levels of private monopolistic power to dangerous global heights, at a time when states, which have been weakened by the forces of globalisation, have less capacity to protect their citizens from the consequences of the exercise of this power.
>
> (Drahos and Braithwaite 2002: 2–3; see also 198–201)

The resulting 'infogopolies' (such as software and media businesses) and 'biogopolies' (such as multinational pharmaceutical companies) wield very substantial power to control access to resources, and to demand high or in some cases extortionate fees for their use.

On the one hand, this could be viewed as the justifiable reward for their investment in innovation. However, the financial returns are often disproportionate, and the level of control over others which can be exercised where there is a significant concentration of intellectual resources can be disturbing. For instance, a pharmaceutical patent gives a monopoly over a product for 20 years, enabling the patent-holder to raise the price of the product far beyond what would be possible if the patent did not exist. This can mean that many drugs are only available to relatively well-off people in wealthy countries, and that treatment is effectively denied to the majority of the world's population, even though the actual cost of producing treatments on a large scale may be minimal. The economic inequalities highlighted by such monopolies are bad enough, but they also have the effect of giving the pharmaceutical companies other forms of power over those unable to purchase medication. The high cost of drugs makes majority-world inhabitants more susceptible to volunteering or being coerced into volunteering for clinical trials of drugs, giving rise to practices that can be understood as a 'new colonialism' (Nundy and Gulhati 2005; cf. Edejer 1999).

Many other problematic cases of intellectual property could be mentioned, and some will be discussed below in relation to the objects of property, or what can be owned. Whether intellectual property is read as giving rise to a new form of feudalism (lord–vassal relationships) or of colonialism (exploitation of and control over geographically limited populations), the point is clear enough: there is immense power associated with large-scale concentrations of abstract resources, and the current global regulatory framework favours 'private' capitalist enterprises over the public domain and over the ethical imperative of substantive equality in fulfilling basic human needs. *Dominium* might be formally distinguished from *imperium*, private ownership from public power, but even a superficial consideration of the material consequences of private ownership tells a quite different story.

WHO? PRIVATE AND COMMON OWNERSHIP

Contemporary liberal emphasis on the autonomous self-owning legal subject with the ability to hold property in various external resources conceals two issues relating to property-owning subjects. First, the class of individual owner, like the class of the legal subject generally, has progressively expanded to become more inclusive at a *de jure* if not a de facto level. More human beings are now capable of holding property rights than ever before, though that does not mean that property ownership has become more equally distributed. Second, however, to what extent is the owner typically a private individual rather than a group, a network, or the public at large? In this section I consider the expansion in the category of individual owners and, more significantly, the historical and ongoing legal and cultural contests between private and common forms of ownership.

Ownership and legal status

The ability to own is first and foremost an incident of legal personality. 'Persons' – both natural and artificial – are entities with rights and responsibilities, one such right being the right to own property. As I indicated above, the owner under Roman law was the person who held the *patria potestas* or paternal power: this was not only power over land and inanimate things, but also power over all animals, family members, slaves, and land. Some aspects of the power were formalised as proprietorial (such as that over slaves and animals) while others developed as personal (such as the power over family members). The operation of this power meant that the male holding the paternal power was also the legal owner of any property held by those within his power, including property possessed by his sons and daughters, and by any grandchildren or great-grandchildren through the male line.[8] Paternal power did not lapse by virtue of children reaching a particular age: it normally only expired with the death of the *paterfamilias*.[9] The Roman era therefore represents a very significant concentration of ownership rights in terms of citizenship, sex, and family position: normally women, slaves, and those within a paternal power were excluded from holding property in their own right, and foreigners were excluded from *dominium*, though they may have had some lesser interests. Even after this general power became differentiated into power over things (including slaves) and power over other family members, the most complete form of ownership, *dominium*, was only available to Roman citizens, reflecting a general discrimination by law between Romans and foreigners.

It is only in the twentieth century that the attributes of legal personality became *formally* (though still not practically) available to most human beings in most contexts, regardless of gender, race, religion, or class. Prior to that time, social hierarchies were often reflected in the law and many people were under severe legal disabilities on account of their religion, ethnicity, or sex (see e.g. Bush 1993; Berns 1993). Of course, this was rarely (if ever) an all-or-nothing equation. In relation simply to the ability to own, for instance, in Britain in the early nineteenth century a Christian male citizen might have the *right* to own property, for instance, but unless he actually did, would not have been entitled to vote. A woman was able to own property if she was not married but, no matter how wealthy, was never entitled to vote. A married woman's legal personality was regarded as being subsumed by the legal being of her husband, meaning in simple

terms that he had absolute rights to her personal property and possessed her real property for the duration of the marriage (see Baker
1990: 552). If a married woman suffered or committed a tort, she
would appear before the court through her husband, but she was, of
course, personally responsible for her own criminal acts (Baker 1990:
557). Foreigners and Jews could own personal, but not real property
(Baker 1990: 531; Bush 1993, 1278). Similar limitations on the personality of certain human beings applied in colonial or former
colonial contexts, though in addition to gender and class hierarchies,
explicitly racial divisions between human beings were legally
enforced. Slavery was permitted in some territories, making human
beings into objects rather than subjects of rights. Indigenous people
in Australia, though technically 'British subjects', clearly did not
hold the same rights as the non-Indigenous. Concepts of natural law
and human rights have resulted in an expansion of the attribution of
legal personality to human beings: human individuals are now formally, if not substantially, equal in rights, including the right to own.

A lasting exception relates to foreigners and foreign corporations:
while Western countries seem only too keen to promote open ownership in expanding or developing economies where national assets
might be purchased cheaply, there is continuing political and social
resistance within many Western countries to foreign ownership of certain resources seen as nationally significant. This is, for instance, manifested by the requirement for some types of foreign investments to be
screened by statutory bodies.[10] Resources closely scrutinised might
include strategic national assets such as airlines, stock exchanges,
and large manufacturing industries; infrastructure such as power
supply and telecommunications; industries with security dimensions
such as ports, weapons manufacturing, and uranium mining; assets
with a significant cultural and political impact such as the print and
electronic media; and of course land, which seems to be the foundation of the spatial identity of the nation itself. In the context of the
often conflicting discourses and legal requirements of free markets,
neo-liberal globalisation, and national security, the question of foreign ownership is, however, a complex and dynamic terrain.

Beyond the private: commons and the public domain

A taxonomy of owners could be constructed in a variety of ways, but
basically the owners of a resource are private individuals, companies,

governments, a limited community, or the public at large (McKean 1992: 251–2).[11] Private individual ownership remains significant in any categorisation, as the section above indicates. But owners are also corporations, shares in which are themselves owned by private individuals, by other companies, or by governments. Such ownership could be classified as 'private', though it may also be 'socialised' or at least dispersed in some sense throughout the population, for instance through pension funds (Murphy et al. 2004: 27). And even though Western liberal governments have in recent decades engaged in widespread divesting of public or government-owned resources under the name of 'privatisation',[12] governments are obviously still significant owners: they own resources such as office buildings essentially privately, they own a (reduced) number of resources as public infrastructure, and environmental resources such as parks and beaches on trust for the public. In countries such as Australia and Canada, Indigenous communities hold native title as a distinct form of property, while other specified groups may hold other forms of common property. Finally, the public at large may be said to 'own' some resources, such as language, the internet, unformed ideas, historical and other facts/news, the air, and the high seas. In relation to resources which *cannot* be appropriated it is perhaps equally true to say that they are owned by everyone, *and* that they represent the antithesis of ownership in that they are non-excludable (Cahir 2004: 624; cf. Gray 1991).

It is possible (and potentially interesting) to consider the differences between individual ownership, corporate ownership, and government/public ownership (cf. Waldron 1988: 38–42). However, the aspects of the ownership matrix I am interested in considering here are forms of collective ownership, the 'commons' and the 'open access' public domain. What is especially interesting from a critical perspective about the public domain and common forms of ownership is that they are in fundamental tension with private ownership, a tension which is played out in ideological, political and social conflicts. Although private (and corporate) property arguably has the upper hand ideologically, a position strengthened by the recent desocialisation and neo-liberalisation of countries such as Britain, Australia and New Zealand, this is nonetheless constantly under challenge from without by emerging non-private resources (especially the internet), as well as from within by its own disintegrating logic (as indicated in Chapters 1 and 2, above).

It is important to distinguish between a notion of the 'commons' where the resource is in the public domain and accessible by all, and one where the resource is shared by some limited group of people, such as a village community, or a subset of people within it (Drahos 1996: 56–8; Ostrom and Hess 2003; cf. Rose 1994: 105–8). Resources in the public domain (open access resources) may be things which cannot be the object of excludable rights because this would be impossible, impractical, or of little benefit: these resources traditionally include language, the air, views, and many social, cultural and environmental resources (Rose 2003: 93–6). In addition some resources such as the high seas, the deep seabed, outer space, and Antarctica are the subject of international agreements which preclude appropriation. Sometimes, in carving out a property right, the state leaves untouched some potentially excludable material: for instance, intellectual property regimes normally leave out what James Boyle calls the 'facts below . . . and ideas above' (Boyle 2003: 39). Or the state takes control of an excludable resource in order that its use will remain public: as Rose comments, such resources 'are overwhelmingly the physical spaces required for mobility' such as roads, rivers, harbours, and airspace (2003: 97). Finally, resources may be inherently excludable, but abandoned or not yet appropriated – typically wild animals and fish are mentioned in this context as the archetypes of the Roman category of *res nullius* (see generally Rose 2003). In addition, much colonialism rested on the concept of *terra nullius* as an inherently excludable but not-yet-appropriated resource (judgement on this latter point being notoriously ignorant of, if not wilfully blind to, the social structures of the First Nations owners and custodians). In the present context resources in outer space may, despite the existence of some rather weak international treaties forbidding its appropriation by states, at some stage constitute a new frontier for the expansion of tangible property rights.

It would be overstating the case to claim that any form of common ownership poses a fundamental threat to private property and its associated cultural discourses of commodification and accumulation. Nonetheless, there has been and still is intense conflict played out in legal, social and political spheres over the extensiveness and nature of rights to take resources out of the commons or out of the public domain for private enjoyment. Public domain goods are regarded as fundamental to a flourishing community: they provide us with the basic ability to move about, to undertake trade and commerce, to engage in recreation, to situate ourselves historically, culturally, or even spiritually (Lange 1981; Rose 2003: 109), to communicate and express ourselves. On the other hand, they are never unregulated, and often tempt commodification, sometimes in the interests of protecting them from overuse. As I will explain, this is a conflict which is increasingly being played out in relation to intellectual resources, where the values of freedom of speech, public participation, and democratic process are often pitted against regulation and propertisation. To make a generalisation which I hope will be at least partly substantiated in what follows: the interests of private ownership continually find new and creative ways to expand the reach of ownership or quasi-ownership control while – on the other hand – technological innovation and political change (for instance concerning cultural heritage or the environment) can undermine the significance of the private sphere, or at least change the terms on which it operates (see generally Cahir 2004).

Old enclosures

The privatisation of commonly used resources is often referred to as 'enclosure': simply, the term 'enclosure' refers to the process of transforming the ownership of a resource from some form of commons or co-ownership to private individual ownership. Normally the term has been used to describe the process of privatising commonly used land in Britain over a period of several centuries, culminating in the age of 'parliamentary enclosures' from the late eighteenth to the late nineteenth century (Daunton 1995: 100–11). In recent decades, critical legal theorists have spoken of a 'second enclosure movement' (Benkler 1999; Boyle 2003), referring to the (metaphorical) landgrab of intellectual resources through various mechanisms of intellectual property. In truth, though, the 'first' enclosure movement was a long and complex transition of law and landscape, starting seriously in the thirteenthth century and continuing until the nineteenth century. And there is arguably more than one 'second' enclosure movement: in addition to intellectual resources being removed from the public domain, natural resources, state monopolies, and other 'common' goods such as urban environments have also been reduced to private ownership (Bottomley 2007: 73–5).

Some of the issues at stake in enclosure can be exemplified by an outline of the 'first' enclosure movement. The enclosed space was often the open fields in which a number of farmers held a small strip of land primarily for growing crops and where agricultural customs determined the use to which the land would be put at any particular time. But enclosure also affected the (originally extensive) waste-lands, traditionally used for grazing animals or gathering firewood (Tate 1967: 32–43; Williams 1970; Taylor 1975: 139–52). Both open fields and wastelands were subject to an intricate system of customary rights or profits held by village inhabitants: such customary interests included the right to glean after the harvest, to graze livestock, to dig turf, or to gather firewood.

According to Daunton, the process of enclosure took three forms: piecemeal enclosure, where individual landholders withdrew (legally or illegally) from any common farming practices; enclosure by private agreement, where the landholders and users agreed to consolidate and rationalise their landholdings; and enclosure by act of parliament, which did not necessarily require the consent of all landholders, and especially not the consent of those who held a mere usufructuary right (Daunton 1995: 100–2). Although the first two methods were often criticised for enforcing the will of the powerful over the poor, it was the third method which generated the most political controversy. This was because it removed a core means of subsistence from villagers who did not have a freehold title to land, but were nonetheless reliant on common use-rights. As Daunton explains:

> Enclosure could spell disaster for landless families who supplemented their income by gathering fuel, grazing a few sheep or a cow, or feeding pigs or geese. Such supplementary income allowed many families to take part in trade and crafts serving the local community, such as carriers, shopkeepers, blacksmiths, and wheelwrights. Enclosure marked the demise of these small rural traders and craftsmen, leaving a more polarized society of landless labourers and farmers.
>
> (Daunton 1995: 107)

Similarly E.P. Thompson says:

> In village after village, enclosure destroyed the scratch-as-scratch-can subsistence economy of the poor. The cottager without legal proof of rights was rarely compensated. The cottager who was able to establish his claim was left with a parcel of land inadequate for subsistence and a disproportionate share of the very high enclosure cost.
>
> (Thompson 1968: 237)

A Scottish variation on the practice of enclosure were the 'clearances' which took place in the highlands from the mid-eighteenth century. As Eric Richards explains, the clearances primarily cleared *people* (and their dwellings) from the highlands in favour of livestock, forcing the highlanders to relocate in towns and cities, or to emigrate (Richards 2000: 5): Richards quotes James Loch – 'one of the main architects of the clearances' – referring to 'the policy of clearing the hills of people, in order to make sheep walks' (Richards 2000: 5). Sheep were more profitable and less labour-intensive than crops, meaning higher rents for the landlords. The Scottish landlords evidently had much greater power to evict their tenants without adhering to the more onerous legal procedures required by enclosure elsewhere, resulting in a process that was 'much harsher than in England' (Richards 2000: 57; cf. Marx 1947: 752–5). Rather than a slow transition in the landscape, its populations, and its uses, the highland clearances were just that: the swift eviction of people from their homes and livelihoods, sometimes accompanied by a plan for their resettlement or emigration (see, for instance, Richards 2000: 153–66).

This brief summary provides only the most elementary outline of the transition from shared occupation and widely distributed rights in relation to land to a more privatised and concentrated form of ownership. It understates a very complex network of transformations in various spheres – notably the social, legal, agricultural, economic and political arenas of life. The history of enclosures and clearances is fraught with controversy and debate, as is the history of scholarship relating to these practices. Were the enclosures an *inevitable* part of agricultural modernisation and rationalisation? Prior to their enclosure, were commonly held resources being subjected to what we now know of as the 'tragedy of the commons', that is, destruction by overuse (cf. Hardin 1968)? To what extent were enclosures resisted by the poor whose lives could be devastated by the changes, and why was there a lack of resistance in some places? Did the rural population necessarily become proletarianised, that is, less independently able to support themselves from the land and more reliant on employment in an increasingly capitalised economy (Marx 1947: 740–57; Turner 1984: 76–7)? Is it accurate to describe the enclosures as 'a plain enough case of class robbery' (Thompson 1968: 237)? In the short term, did the number of small landholders rise or decline (Daunton 1995: 108)?

These are not questions which can be addressed in any detail here.

What I would like briefly to outline is what enclosure meant (and means) in socio-political discourse: how has it been interpreted as part of some very broad economic and social changes. Enclosure is sometimes understood to represent a transition from communalism to individualism, a 'popular' theory of transition in land ownership which Maitland said 'has the great merit of being vague and elastic' (Maitland 1897: 341). On one level the narrative of common to private seems correct: a resource such as a wasteland might have been subject to a 'right of common' to graze animals, held by a number of local villagers. But this did not mean that the community at large owned the land: rather that a number of people held a right in common, a profit, which could be enforced against the landowner, for instance the lord of the local manor (Drahos 1996: 56; cf. Maitland 1897: 341). The resource was used in a defined way by a defined number of people who held the right either by grant or by immemorial custom, and not by the public at large (not, for instance, by the neighbouring villagers).[13] As Maitland argues, medieval modes of distributing interests in land cannot be easily equated with modern concepts: the idea that land ownership has moved from communal to individual is at best a generalisation, and begs the questions of exactly who held what, and whether it really amounted to ownership in the modern sense at all (Maitland 1897: 340–56; see also Daunton 1995: 104). Whatever the legal nature of ownership prior to enclosure, however, it does seem obvious that the movement both reflected and reinforced a strengthening ideology of private ownership together with its notions of boundedness, exclusivity, and the concentration of rights in single individuals rather than their distribution among numbers of proprietors.

For proponents and defenders of the movement, enclosure has often been seen through the lens of economic efficiency (Brace 2001). From this perspective, enclosure was simply a necessary condition of agricultural progress and improvement: enclosure allowed agriculture to take advantage of technological innovations, it facilitated large-scale farming, and therefore ensured a much more robust supply of agricultural products. There was also a correlation between the strengthening concept of concentrated private ownership, and the colonial mentality that territory was a vital resource needing subjugation. Nationalist propaganda in favour of enclosure equated the domestic privatisation and 'improvement' of land with war and colonial conquest. In 1803 Sir John Sinclair made the connection explicitly:

> We have begun another campaign against the foreign enemies of
> the country . . . why should we not attempt a campaign also
> against our great domestic foe, I mean the hitherto unconquered
> sterility of so large a proportion of the surface of the kingdom?
> Let us not be satisfied with the liberation of Egypt, or the subju-
> gation of Malta, but let us subdue Finchley Common; let us
> conquer Hounslow Heath, let us compel Epping Forest to submit
> to the yoke of improvement.
>
> (quoted in Williams 1970: 57)

As we will see, critics of modern enclosures also draw attention to
the relationship between huge concentrations of private resources
and new forms of colonialism and imperialism.

In contrast to the narratives of economic efficiency, national progress, and subjugation of vital resources, critics of enclosure have
regretted the enlargement of the realm of private property which it
represents. For many, the movement towards a fully capitalist economy was hardly one to be celebrated, and led to the individualisation
and alienation of the population. Karl Marx, for one, was in no
doubt about the relationship between the changes in land-holding
which had occurred from the late middle ages and the proletarianisa-
tion of the rural poor:

> The spoilation of the church's property, the fraudulent alien-
> ation of the State domains, the robbery of the common lands,
> the usurpation of feudal and clan property, and its transform-
> ation into modern private property under circumstances of reck-
> less terrorism, were just so many idyllic methods of primitive
> accumulation. They conquered the field for capitalistic agri-
> culture, made the soil part and parcel of capital, and created for
> the town industries the necessary supply of a 'free' and outlawed
> proletariat.
>
> (Marx 1947: 757)

As already indicated, after enclosure the poor found it much more
difficult to live independently by supplementing employment or trade-
based income with grazing sheep or gleaning after the harvest. They
became more reliant on wages and, when farm work was not available (e.g. when the demand for labour was reduced by efficient farming, or by replacing crops with livestock), they were forced to look
for work in the towns, particularly in the rapidly growing industrial

sector. Whatever the overall economic benefits, enclosure was certainly not without its victims.

New enclosures

Enclosures in Britain were effectively ended by the Commons Act 1876, though 'the destruction of the ancient manorial structure of villages had by then been almost completed' (Simpson 1986: 261). There was very little left to enclose. However, the notion of enclosure, meaning generally the reduction of common resources to private property, is far from redundant: the conflict between common and private is still being played out with great intensity across the world. However, enclosure no longer refers only to the privatisation and exclusive ownership of land. Contemporary scholars have written of a 'second enclosure movement' (Boyle 2003; Benkler 1999) in the area of intellectual property law. Put simply, the second enclosure movement takes intellectual resources out of the commons or the public domain and makes them into private property: 'once again things that were formerly thought of as either common property or uncommodifiable are being covered with new, or newly extended, property rights' (Boyle 2003: 37).

Defining the 'public domain' in intellectual resources is notoriously difficult, but clearly it includes a variety of cultural, scientific, and historical 'objects', as Tyler Ochoa explains:

> The public domain is something that we enjoy every day without thinking about it. We take it for granted that the plays of Shakespeare and the symphonies of Beethoven are in the public domain and may be freely copied, adapted, and performed by anyone. Our theatres are filled with movies and musicals based on public domain works. We daily use technology derived from earlier inventions, such as the car, the airplane, the telephone, and the computer. We understand intuitively that any scientist may rely on Newton's laws of motion or Einstein's theory of relativity as he or she sees fit. We use common words that once were brand names such as aspirin, cellophane, thermos, and escalator. Students and scholars debate historical events, ranging from the origins of man to the impeachment of President Clinton.
>
> (Ochoa 2003: 215)

Whereas the old enclosure movement usually referred to the enclosure of commons in which a limited number of people had rights, the new enclosure movement is normally envisaged as the encroachment of private interests on this open, public domain.

Sometimes the new enclosure occurs through the opening up of an intellectual terrain, a formerly undiscovered intellectual *res nullius* which, once found, can – like the *terra nullius* of colonial times – be appropriated: the documenting and patenting of human DNA sequences is a good example of a relatively newly discovered intellectual *res* (Boyle 2003: 37). (The genome is also an intellectual thing which many have argued should not be capable of private ownership: arguably it 'belongs' to all humanity and not to a few enterprising corporations and, moreover, permitting ownership blurs the line of person and thing which is (it is said) vital to human dignity: see Roberts 1987; Thomas et al. 1996).

In other cases, 'enclosure' refers to a progressive encroachment of the 'territory' of intellectual property into previously public or untested spheres – for instance, the use of copyright to protect compilations of facts such as telephone directories and other databases (Boyle 2003: 39), or the restriction on the use of historical figures under an extended right of personality (Lange 1981). And sometimes enclosure occurs by the enlargement of an existing intellectual property right, for instance adding 20 years to the copyright term, so that it takes longer for a literary work to enter the public domain. A slightly different category of case concerns 'biopiracy', which involves patents being claimed, usually by multinational pharmaceutical companies or agribusinesses, for traditional knowledges (Shiva 1997; 2001; Mgbeoji 2006; Roht-Arriaza 1997). This is a special case because it does not concern intellectual objects being enclosed from the Western public domain, but is arguably a new form of colonialism: a profitable taking of 'unowned' or 'unexploited' resources from Indigenous or other 'long term occupants' (Heald 2003) who do not share the individual private property mentality of Western capitalist economies.

In most of these cases, the enlargement of the private domain is at the expense of open, public access to intellectual resources. Of course, as Boyle argues, the problem is not simply that the terrain of intellectual property is becoming progressively larger, while the public domain shrinks. Assuming property is to be recognised at all, the public and private domains of intellectual resources need to be held in balance. Indeed one of the motivations behind a limited copyright term and a limited patent term is to ensure that *both* the creator/inventor and the public benefit: without patent law, inventors might be more inclined to keep their inventions secret, whereas the patent ensures that after a term of years it will be openly useful (Rose 2003). The problem therefore may be that enclosure is occurring as a knee-jerk response to the perceived threat posed by increasingly available and cheap technological methods of using and reproducing intellectual resources. With the internet, public access is potentially far more extensive than ever: a 'shared' book or music file available on the internet can be accessed virtually freely by an unlimited number of people. (And I note in passing the semiotic contest between 'sharing' something and 'stealing' it: the same act of copying may be characterised in either way, depending on one's perspective.) The enclosure of such resources via increasingly strict intellectual property regimes occurs without adequate debate and information, and without proper investigation into whether the claimed reasons for expansion of private rights are really good justifications. It has also been facilitated by a very strong cultural and political narrative of private property, and in the absence of an equally strong narrative of the commons or the public domain (counteracting this, see Lange 1981).

In the context of tangible resources such as land, one justification for private as opposed to common or public rights relates to the so-called 'tragedy of the commons' – the idea that the value of a commonly owned resource will be destroyed or diminished by overuse (Hardin 1968). The argument has provided some useful rhetorical tools for those interested in increasing the domain of private ownership. But it may be simplistic. Even in relation to tangible resources, some have argued that the tragedy of the commons has been greatly exaggerated: in cases of 'managed commons' accessible to a limited number of people under defined circumstances, it is not necessarily the case that common rights lead to more wasteful and less sustainable behaviour than private rights. In many instances well-managed commons may be far preferable (Berkes et al. 1989; Ostrom et al 1999; Rose C. 1999). There are also plenty of examples of degradation of land by private owners interested in short-term gain. The 'tragedy of the commons' narrative applies more easily to openly accessible public resources, rather than to resources accessed and managed in common by a defined group. In times when pollution was unregulated, air and water quality were undoubtedly diminished by open public and corporate access to the atmosphere and waterways. On a global scale, the environment is diminished by the unrestrained, or barely restrained, release of greenhouse gases.

While the concept of the tragedy of the commons is of reduced relevance in the case of 'common property regimes', as many commentators have observed, it makes even less sense in the context of intellectual property (Boyle 2003: 41–4; Rose 2003: 90). Intellectual resources cannot be diminished by overuse: no matter how many times a book is read or how many times a piece of music is played or copied, the original *res* covered by the property right is not diminished. What *may* be reduced, if unlimited use or copying of an intellectual resource takes place, is the creator's or owner's ability to benefit economically from the resource. This is a matter of the fair distribution of the benefits to be gained from intellectual resources: where should the boundary between intellectual property and the public domain be set? In any event, there may also be economic benefits to be gained from the additional visibility caused by less restricted use, a matter which, as Boyle notes, has not been soundly investigated (2003: 43). In other words, perhaps it is simplistic to think of the division of the intellectual domain into public and private as a zero-sum game. The value of a resource to both the public *and* the private owner may be increased by weakening rather than strengthening property rights: there is little evidence either way (but much ideology).

A more serious justification for intellectual property rights (and their extension) relates to providing incentives for creativity and innovation: it is argued that without property rights, there would be little reward and thus no incentive for people to create intellectual resources or for companies to invest in innovation. This justification presumes that creative behaviour is highly rational, in the economic sense, highly individualised, and self-interested. As many have commented, it tends to reify and romanticise an authorial genius who is, after all, a modern invention, as the source of artistic originality. Martha Woodmansee describes a change in consciousness from the Renaissance to the early modern period: from being a craftsman channelling an external inspiration (e.g. from God), the artist became an originator with their own internal inspiration (Woodmansee 1984).[14] It is also based on the idea that the author/artist will be the main beneficiary of their inventiveness, which is often not the case, large profits going to those publishers or music distributors who end up holding the copyright. On the other hand, the history of open-source software, of open-access intellectual spaces such as the

Creative Commons, and of commonly accessible resources from individual weblogs to large-scale enterprises such as Wikipedia, suggests otherwise: even without private rewards or recognition, there are plenty of non-economic incentives for creativity and for the development of new forms of communal innovation (Cahir 2004; Boyle 2003).[15] Again, the issue is not really whether or not to reward creativity through intellectual property: most scholars agree that this is appropriate to some degree. The issue is rather where to draw the line in order to optimise both creativity *and* the public's access to resources, and to avoid simply enriching the interests of large businesses at the expense of the overall public good.

Because of the subject matter of this book, I have emphasised the distinction between intellectual property and its other, the public domain where property rights do not exist. However, as some scholars have argued, this focus on intellectual property underestimates the broader contexts within which information circulates. Just as there are non-property regulations governing tangible public domain resources, there are many ways in which information is protected and controlled which are not based in intellectual property: some obvious examples are the control on communication through defamation, trade secrets, and confidential communications. Judith Bannister has argued that it is simplistic to think of information in terms of a dichotomy between private property and public domain, and that much information takes the form of 'overlapping managed commons' – that is plural and overlapping spheres of information controlled and accessible by a limited group of people for specific purposes (Bannister 2006; see also Ostrom and Hess 2003).

Some forms of information control are proprietary in the sense that they establish exclusive and alienable rights, and are classified as forms of intellectual property. In other cases, a property-effect may arise from the exercise of non-proprietorial forms of control. Importantly, despite the attractive rhetoric connecting the public domain with freedom of expression and participatory democracy, in some instances a managed commons may be preferable for furthering the interests of social justice, accountable bureaucracy and democratic participation. Bannister demonstrates this with reference to forms of Australian Indigenous knowledge where secrecy or limited communication may be required for cultural reasons. While such secret knowledges may look incoherent from a Western perspective, the reasons for protecting them are arguably just as strong as the commercial and other reasons advanced for controlling trade secrets, intellectual property, political secrets, and other commonly controlled information.

WHAT? PERSONS AND THINGS

It is evident from the discussion in the first two parts of this chapter that the nature of the ownership, the identities of the owners and the objects which can be owned are mutually constructing and intertwined. For instance, in the common law women and children have not technically been regarded as alienable objects of property, though they have been regarded as existing within the paternal power of their husbands and fathers. They are also often symbolically and socially objects rather than subjects, making them as near as possible to property without actually being it. The extended meanings of property shape who can legitimately own and who can be comprehended as a political and social subject. Similarly, the debates over the balancing of private interests against the public domain are in part about the sorts of content which can and cannot be privately owned, indicating the relationship between the type of owner (or whether one exists at all) and the owned object. And as I have tried to show, there is nothing natural or pre-social about the constructions and distributions of power, rights, and objects of property – these distributions are entirely the product of prevailing socio-political and economic influences within a historical context.

The scholarship on new enclosures and the public domain can give the impression that an ever-increasing slice of the finite pie which is the world's tangible and intellectual resources is being reduced to property. In some contexts this is undoubtedly true, but a broad historical perspective presents a more complicated picture of shifting demarcations between objects and subjects of property, between public, common and private domains, and between things which are regarded as available for human exploitation and those which are not. In this final section of the chapter, I will review some transitions in the objects of property, focusing first on the demarcations between subjects and objects of property rights, and finally mentioning one or two of the more controversial cases of which resources can become property.

Human objects

I have already considered the legal, social, and symbolic dimensions of the status of wives and of children. Both cases demonstrate the sway of the structure of property in a familial, cultural setting which (unevenly) reproduces and is reproduced by the legal consciousness. But women and children are obviously not the only human entities to have fallen on the wrong side of the subject/object divide. This is clearest in relation to the millions of slaves who, where slavery was recognised, were seen simply as property, chattels. It was in parallel with the formal abolition of slavery that the strong narrative of the separation of persons and property arose.

Prior to the abolition of slavery, there was little legal contradiction in seeing persons as fungible things, that is, as objects which could be bought and sold. In Aristotle's *Politics*, for instance, there is a distinction between 'natural' and 'conventional' slavery. Natural slavery is simply the condition of some people who, in his view, are most suited for servitude: 'It is clear then that by nature some are free, others slaves, and that for these it is both right and expedient that they should be seen as slaves' (Aristotle 1962: 34). Aristotle's strained and defensive justifications reveal that, even in an age when slavery was common, the ethics and acceptability of slavery were questioned.[16] Aristotle's 'conventional' slavery was the consequence of victory in war: in the ancient world it was accepted by many that the victors had the right to enslave the vanquished (ibid: 35). Some 900 or so years after the time of Aristotle, the *Institutes* commissioned by the Roman jurist and emperor Justinian said that slavery was a part of the law of nations or *ius gentium*, but against the law of nature – 'for, by natural law, originally, all men were born free' (Thomas 1975: 5). Pre-liberal writers such as Locke, Hobbes and Montesquieu also rejected the idea that slavery was part of the natural law or condition of human beings. Locke, for instance, argued against natural and conventional slavery on the basis that people were naturally 'free from any Superior Power on Earth', that any political power had to be established by consent or compact, and that a person could not consent to their own enslavement: 'Nobody can give more Power than he has himself; and he that cannot take away his own Life, cannot give another power over it' (Locke 1988: §§22 and 23). Nonetheless, there were qualifications, slavery being tolerated by these writers in some, albeit limited, circumstances (Smith 1992: 1784 9).

As a practice, the institution of slavery has varied enormously through time and across geographical locations, with the one constant being that it regards human beings – in their entire physical being – as capable of being owned. From ancient and medieval forms of slavery through to the transatlantic trade in African people, and the enslavement of Jews and Romani by the Nazis in the Second World War, slavery has been underpinned by different ideologies: slaves could be seen as part of the normal social order, as an offshore means of accumulating wealth and supporting national economies, as an expression of 'natural' racial differences, and/or as a source of absolutely disposable labour. The very concept of a slave is of a human as property, but – as is currently the case with animals – the object of property could be protected in some way without being the holder of rights. At times, legal regimes allowed masters to kill their slaves, while at other times and in other places, killing and other forms of cruelty were not permitted (though whether infringements were actually punished by law was a different matter). Emancipation was sometimes permitted, sometimes not. At times, slaves were educated and respected for their intellect and creativity, at other times regarded as sub-human.

The history of slavery is not, however, simply one of gradual improvement and enlightenment. Some of the worst abuses of human beings were indeed associated with converging Enlightenment ideologies: in particular the intersection of racism and capitalism associated with the slave trade of the early modern era. Ancient and medieval slave practices were by no means more barbaric than the transatlantic slave trade of the fifteenth century onwards (see generally Brooks 2003). The transatlantic trade was underpinned by early and rampant capitalism: although ancient slaves were tradable commodities, the later slave trade brought a previously unknown scale and profitability to the practice (Carrington 2003). Moreover, the early modern slave trade was based upon (and reinforced) an emerging racist ideology which regarded white Christian Europeans as the natural masters of other races, and, in particular, regarded Africans as barely human. For while Aristotle thought that Greeks were the 'proper' rulers over others and that 'barbarian and slave are by nature identical' (Aristotle 1962: 27), this seems to be a claim based more on the relatively advanced nature of Greek civilisation, rather than one based on race or ethnicity. In contrast, the Enlightenment produced conditions under which the natural sciences and their taxonomic approach to all physical things could flourish: in this environment, natural scientists and philosophers produced hierarchical classifications of race according to biological characteristics (Bernasconi 2001: 11–36) which supported an ideology of European/white moral and intellectual superiority. And while liberalism with its focus upon natural freedom and equality eventually spawned the European movement for the abolition of slavery, early liberal thought seemed quite content with so-called 'natural' distinctions among human beings. (It is, apparently, debatable whether the abolitionist movement was really primarily responsible for the abolition of the slave trade or whether this was equally the result of its declining profitability: cf. Carrington 2003.)

While national laws generally forbid ownership of humans, a wide variety of informal and illegal practices nonetheless condemn many human beings to slavery. As a United Nations Fact Sheet explains:

> The word 'slavery' today covers a variety of human rights violations. In addition to traditional slavery and the slave trade, these abuses include the sale of children, child prostitution, child pornography, the exploitation of child labour, the sexual mutilation of female children, the use of children in armed conflicts, debt bondage, the traffic in persons and in the sale of human organs, the exploitation of prostitution, and certain practices under *apartheid* and colonial régimes.[17]

Thus although slavery has been outlawed in international law for some time,[18] it would be quite wrong to suggest that humans are therefore no longer property (see also Rassam 1999).

The general principle, if not the practice, is that human beings should not be property. This has not prevented dead, detached or externalisable parts of human beings from becoming property under certain circumstances.[19] A corpse or parts of a corpse may in some circumstances be regarded as property, for instance, where it has been transformed from a mere body to something else (Davies and Naffine 2001: 112–15). Sale of human organs is illegal in most parts of the world, but that has not stopped an extensive black market in organs. However, certain body parts – especially the renewable parts like hair and even blood – are sometimes legally regarded as objects of property (Chambers 2001: 20–4). Novel practices, not quite amounting to recognition of property rights, can also arise. For instance, the United Kingdom Human Fertilisation and Embryology Authority has recently licensed an 'egg-sharing' arrangement, whereby a research team will pay part of the costs of IVF treatment in exchange for women donating their eggs: fresh eggs are especially in demand for stem cell research.[20] Intellectual property in person-related entities is also possible. DNA sequences have been patented in large numbers.[21] And interestingly, Canada and many US states recognise personality rights as property. If I happened to be a celebrity, I would be able to exclude others from making use of my image, voice or other distinctive personality traits to further their own commercial interests (Dangelo 1989; Singer 1991; Frow 1995). In the UK and Australia, some similar protection exists under the tort of 'passing off',[22] but this is much more limited.

Without going into further detail about these matters, it is nonetheless clear that the distinction between persons and property, even as reflected in law, is not a bright line, but is rather contextual and flexible. Several processes can alter the essential humanity of an object so that it becomes something other and objective, subject to appropriation – a dead body or body part can be transformed, a live body part can be detached, a personality can be abstracted and reified, their DNA extracted and mapped. Persons and property are 'fabricated' according to different contexts, discourses, and practices – legal and otherwise (Pottage and Mundy 2004).

Non-human objects

Apart from human beings, their tissue, DNA, and personality attributes, much of the current debate of objects of property has focused on intellectual property and the new problems raised by digitisation and the internet. As I have indicated, much of the controversy in this context is about the proper balance between public access and private rights. In addition to the categories of human and intellectual things, there are a number of other objects with a debatable status as property or potential property. Kevin Gray has argued that in order to become property in law, a thing must be physically, legally, and morally excludable (Gray 1991).[23] For instance, the oxygen we breathe and a publicly available view cannot become property because it is not physically practicable to exclude people from the use of such resources. Everyday language (as opposed to business names and trademarks) is an essential part of the human commons, necessary for human co-existence, and it would therefore be immoral to regard it as property. (On the other hand, this is an evaluation of language which cannot be regarded as universal. It has been stated, for instance, in relation to the Kaurna language of the Indigenous people of what is now Adelaide, South Australia, that it is 'owned' 'in the same way that songs, ceremonies and land are owned'.[24]) Gray's is a very helpful and interesting analysis, particularly as it concerns tangible resources: however, especially in the category of 'moral excludability', there is much controversy about what ought to be included and what standards of 'morality' apply. There is a good deal of variation over time, as we have seen in relation to human beings. Should land be regarded as private property? And what about water, or outer space? Are these resources too environmentally and socially important to be regarded as purely fungible? Marx argued that the means of capitalist production should not be privately owned, since this leads to the exploitation of workers. And there has been very significant concern over the move towards private ownership of social infrastructure, such as utilities providing energy, telecommunications, or transport. The categories of what can and should be owned are somewhat transient, and often controversial.

Animals are another special case. Typically they are regarded as property, but might be regarded as having ethical claims of their own. As Ariel Simon notes: '[i]t is difficult to imagine that anyone would claim that a pet monkey and an inanimate carbon rod hold equal moral weight' (Simon 2006: 5). At the same time, 'fish are clearly not human beings' (ibid: 7). But fish, monkeys, chairs, and carbon rods are equally regarded by law as property and although the animals might be protected from extreme cruelty by legislation, they are nonetheless essentially fungible. There is a 'Great Legal Wall' (Wise 1999: 61) separating humans from non-humans, a position which has been challenged on environmental grounds, and also on the grounds that animals should be regarded as subjects, not objects, of rights.

FUTURES OF PROPERTY

Is history repeating itself? In this chapter we have seen that, for some, feudalism is entering a modern iteration, while the process and ideology of enclosure has been extended from literal landscapes to intellectual landscapes. Slavery has been formally abolished internationally, but that has not meant an end to the practice or to more subtle blurring of the person–property distinction. Whole classes of people have escaped formal identification as property only to find that they are still culturally commodified. Things move in and out of the category of objects of property. Old forms and ideas reappear in new contexts. On the other hand, to reduce property histories to a repetitive cycle would be to underestimate the political and intellectual conflicts which property attracts. It would also neglect the new resources (such as the internet and culture) and new social concerns (such as environmentalism and globalisation) which change the terms upon which these contests are played out. The future is influenced but not determined by the past. In Chapter 5 I will consider how some of these contemporary questions might hold promise for a different understanding of property.

Notes

1 By the term 'racial capital', I mean the racial equivalent of what Skeggs refers to as 'cultural capital', that is, a privilege which has an exchange value or, as Cheryl Harris termed it, 'whiteness as property' (Skeggs 2004; Harris 1993). See also Chapter 2, above.

2 And even now, marital rape is sometimes regarded as a lesser crime than other forms of rape. See generally *R v R* [1992] 1 AC 599; *R v L* (1991) 174 CLR 379; Hasday 2000; Warner 2000.

3 This was despite infamous pronouncements such as that in *Mawgridge* (1707) 84 ER 1107 at 1115: 'jealousy is the rage of a man and adultery is the highest invasion of property'.

4 The quotation is from 'Directions for Obedience Government in Dangerous or Doubtful Times' originally published in 1652 and republished in Filmer 1949.

5 Unproved allegations also recently suggested that nominations for peerages might have been exchanged for substantial loans to a political party.

6 Leader, 'Slow Exit', *Guardian*, Saturday 5 August 2006, viewed 7 August 2006 at www.guardian.co.uk/commentisfree/story/0,,1837774,00.html.

7 In March 2007 the House of Commons voted in favour of a fully elected House of Lords, while the House of Lords voted in favour of a fully appointed House. It is yet to be seen how the newest round of reforms will play out.

8 The children of a daughter (and their possessions) would normally be in the power of her husband or his father.

9 Or by the operation of law where, as the *Twelve Tables* said, if the father sold his son three times, the son would be free.

10 Australia, for instance, has a Foreign Acquisitions and Takeovers Act 1975, and the Australian state of Queensland has a Foreign Ownership of Land Register Act 1988, under which all land owned by foreigners must be registered as such. See also the Investment Canada Act 1985.

11 Cahir (2004: 620) distinguishes three types of property – 'private, public,

and common', or ownership by a 'private legal entity', ownership by the state, and the situation which arises where there is an absence of rights of exclusion, i.e. both the negation of property and a positive public domain. This division, while perfectly reasonable, highlights the difficulty of categorising types of property. Some writers insist upon reserving the term 'commons' to a resource accessible by a limited group of people (which I think Cahir would define under 'private', since a right of exclusion exists, cf. Rose 2003: 106), while the term 'public domain', as used for instance by Lange (1981), is distinct from Cahir's public (i.e. government) property, referring instead to what Cahir calls the 'information commons'. Because I am highlighting the various constructions of the *owner*, I have adopted a different taxonomy: basically that proposed by McKean (1992: 251–2). I refer to state or government property (some of which is private and some of which overlaps with the public domain), limited commons, and the public domain.

12 I recall the bumper sticker (source unknown) which said 'Privatisation: why buy what you already own?'

13 An interesting aside is that while enclosure meant the decline of such rights of common, it also assisted the rise of easements, since rights of way – previously unnecessary in the open countryside – were needed to ensure the ability of people to pass through privately owned fields (Simpson 1986: 261–2).

14 A very interesting and extensive literature, which I do not have space to consider here, illustrates that the 'author' is essentially a modern invention. For two early pieces see Woodmansee 1984; Foucault 1979, and for more recent discussions see Aoki 1996 and Sherman and Bentley 1999: 35–7, who also consider in detail the early justifications for recognising property in literature.

15 There are other justifications for recognising intellectual property – for instance, that we ought to own the products of our mental labour (just as we ought to own the products of our physical labour); or that we simply own them by occupation: Sherman and Bently 1999: 20–4.

16 As Sinclair points out in his note to this section (Aristotle, Penguin edition, 1962) Aristotle has not provided anything like a convincing argument that some slavery is natural, he has merely asserted that people are needed to do menial and physical tasks.

17 Office of the High Commissioner for Human Rights, Fact Sheet No. 14 (1991) 'Contemporary Forms of Slavery' available at http://www.unhchr. ch/html/menu6/2/fs14.htm, last viewed 14 April 2007.

18 E.g. The Universal Declaration of Human Rights 1948 Article 4: 'No-one shall be held in slavery or servitude: slavery and the slave trade shall be prohibited in all their forms.'

19 Again, there is a very extensive and fascinating literature on this topic.

20 See Press Release, University of Newcastle, 'Egg-sharing' go ahead for stem-cell researchers' 27 July 2006 http://www.ncl.ac.uk/press.office/ press.release/content.phtml?ref=1154008083, viewed 14 April 2007.

21 See, for instance, *Moore v Regents of the University of California* (1990) 793 P 2d 479.

22 The wrong of 'passing off' in this context is not appropriation of the

property in an image, but rather the false representation that a person endorses a product.

23 For the sake of simplicity I have omitted discussion of Gray's legal excludability, which is inherently more complicated conceptually.

24 Rob Amery and Kaurna Language and Language Ecology Class, University of Adelaide, quoted in Janke 1998: 20.

Chapter 4

Theories

INTRODUCTION

In Chapter 2 I outlined aspects of the cultural meanings of property, illustrating how it acts as a metaphor for ideas of the self, knowledge and law. In Chapter 3 some of the historical transitions in the legal idea of property were considered: the transitions I described concerned the changing shape of property and, in particular, its shifting relationship to various forms of power, the changing identities of property owners and some important shifts in what can be regarded as an object of property. These historical transitions were motivated and accompanied by a combination of economic, cultural, ideological and political factors, including rising individualism, gender and racial equality, the desire for economic security, corporate power, and secularism.

In the scheme I have adopted in this book, philosophical theories constitute a third side of the 'cultural matrix' of property. The philosophy of property is normally taken to involve two key issues: first, the nature of property – 'what is property?'; and second, the moral or other justifications for property. In this chapter I focus mainly upon the second of these questions; although obviously the first question is often embedded in it (it is difficult to justify something without first knowing what is being justified). Given the foundational nature of defining property (and the ultimate impossibility of doing so), I have considered some (admittedly minimal) aspects of this question in Chapter 1.

This chapter will look at two well-known theories of private property, beginning with what has become the most influential and controversial approach to property in those parts of the world influenced by English law and colonialism, that of John Locke and his

Second Treatise of Government. Following this consideration of Locke and his contested place in the development of property-thought, I will turn to the German philosopher G.W.F. Hegel, whose *Philosophy of Right* provides a view of property which shares some similarities to Locke's approach, but is also distinct in some fundamental points. Hegel's work has been adapted in some interesting ways by several contemporary critical legal theorists.

LOCKE, LIBERTY, AND THE COLONIES

In the last decades of the twentieth century there has been a revival of interest in Locke as a political writer, rather than simply as an abstract philosopher (Arneil 1994). In this respect, two features of Locke's own life have come to the fore: first, his association with a radical (early liberal) politics which aimed to broaden the base of political participation (Schochet 1989); second, his theoretical and personal interest in justifying colonial expansion. Both of these issues raise very complicated questions about Locke's place in the context of seventeenth-century (and subsequent) political thought (Tully 1993). Looking at matters solely from a twenty-first-century perspective, Locke's political liberalism regarding domestic affairs sits uncomfortably with his strong defence of highly exploitative colonial practices. In the following discussion I am not going to attempt to understand Locke within his own political context: this is a matter best left to the historians of political thought. Rather I will confine my discussion to some critical questions about the continuing resonance of Locke's views on property, highlighting in particular some of the tensions and contradictions which are evident, especially as it relates to colonial expansion and current imperialism.

It might be overstating matters to claim that Locke's theory remains directly influential on cultural and legal understandings of property, in the way that it directly influenced colonial policy in the eighteenth and nineteenth centuries. However, it is no overstatement to say that it represents a political lexicon and ideology which is a key element of Western liberalism. As James Tully puts it:

> Three hundred years after its publication the *Two Treatises* continues to present one of the major political philosophies of the modern world. By this I mean it provides a set of concepts we standardly use to represent and reflect on contemporary politics.

This arrangement of concepts is not the only form of reflection on modern politics, not our 'horizon' so to speak, but it is a familiar and customary one.

(Tully 1993: 137)

In relation to property, for instance, Locke's work gives philosophical credibility to several concepts: self-ownership; property as the reward for individual labour; the economic benefits of enclosing the commons; and a moral argument that land must be cultivated or put to industrial use to benefit humankind. These ideas have entered the narrative of liberalism and are regularly deployed by politicians and political commentators. They are certainly not the only concepts regarding property in circulation, and often enter into competition with ideas derived from environmental, socialist, or First Nations perspectives. Nonetheless, the Lockean concepts remain very powerful.

Locke: The *Second Treatise*

Locke's *Second Treatise of Government*, and in particular Chapter V, 'Of Property', has been the subject of very extensive scholarly debates. Despite much criticism of the theory put forward by Locke, and despite the limitations which he placed upon acquisition of property, the theory seems to have an intrinsic appeal. This appeal is perhaps derived from the fact that the theory is based on rewarding labour, which seems intuitively just. The theory posits property not as something which is derived from a person's God-given or natural status, but rather as something which can be acquired by anyone, and even accumulated. These elements of Locke's thought must have seemed very attractive to the emerging capitalist, new landowning, and colonialist classes of the late seventeenth century. At the same time it offered nothing more than grand rhetoric for those without the capacity to grasp new opportunities for accumulation, and even less for those dispossessed by colonial expansion. As Lebovics put it:

Commentators have noted the curious ambiguity of Locke's political writings which permitted him to justify the actions of rapacious and rebellious men of wealth of his and later ages and at the same time hold forth a promise of unprecedented political participation for the many.

(Lebovics 1986: 579)

As was so often the case in the development of liberal thought, the extension of political power, property and privilege was incremental: for Locke, it did not apply to women (Pateman 1988; Arneil 2001), it is doubtful whether it applied to the working classes (Schochet 1989), and it openly accepted the exploitation of slaves and those still living in what he perceived as a 'state of nature'. The liberalism of equality for rational individuals and the illiberalism of discriminating against those who are presumed not to fit this norm, are two sides of the one coin (Parekh 1995).

In Chapter 3 I discussed the enclosure movement which took place in Britain from the middle ages through to the nineteenth century, and outlined current concerns about a second enclosure movement taking place in the sphere of intellectual property. Locke's approach to property is first and foremost a theory of and justification for enclosure, not only in Britain, not only in the so-called 'new' world, but everywhere, anywhere and for all time. Or, as one commentator has put it, Locke's was a 'notion of appropriation' rather than a 'theory of property' (Thomas 2003: 30).

Like most Enlightenment philosophers, Locke's thought was intended to be universal, but it was nonetheless a Eurocentric universalism which assumed that ownership involved fencing and using an item (in this case land), that political organisation took a particular institutionalised form, and that accumulation was not only a natural desire but a God-given duty (Parekh 1995). Like the practical and legal acts of enclosure discussed in Chapter 4, Locke's theoretical enclosures start with the commons and the presumption of a state of nature: in the Christian world inhabited by Locke the commons were a gift from God, available to all in the state of nature, but ultimately to be used for the benefit and prosperity of 'mankind'. Evidently, Locke's 'commons' were somewhat akin to an unlimited realm where everything was *res* or *terra nullius*. It was not a protected public domain, nor a limited commons, since objects could be removed from the commons without the consent or even the participation of other 'commoners'. This is important, because ultimately it gave colonialists the power to appropriate land and resources without the consent of native populations. In Locke's state of nature the world was, to be blunt, up for grabs – as long as it was grabbed in the right way.

The right way, as is well known, relates to the use of labour, as Locke argued in one of the most famous passages from the *Second Treatise*:

> Though the Earth, and all inferior Creatures be common to all Men, yet every Man has a *Property* in his own *Person*. This no body has any Right to but himself. The *Labour* of his Body, and the *Work* of his Hands, we may say, are properly his. Whatsoever then he removes out of the State that Nature hath provided, and left it in, he hath mixed his *Labour* with, and joined to it something that is his own, and thereby makes it his *Property*.
>
> (Locke 1988: 287–8)

Because it relies upon the so-called natural law principles of self-preservation and self-ownership – rather than upon political or legal society – such a form of appropriation can take place without the consent of others, at least where there is no recognised political society to regulate ownership (ibid: 286). This right of appropriation is, however, limited by two provisos – the appropriator must leave 'enough, and as good' for others (ibid: 288), and that it is not permissible to appropriate more than it is possible to use without spoilage (ibid: 295). However, it is legitimate to exchange a thing which spoils for one which does not, meaning that this second proviso (which would otherwise prohibit over-accumulation) did not apply once money was invented (ibid: 300–1). Locke viewed money simply as the means of storing an excess without wasting it or injuring others: thus, once accumulation becomes possible by storing money, the foundations and indeed justifications for inequality are laid (Bell et al. 2004).

Liberty and the individual

Locke's person was not owned by another, but by the self. The person is, and is not, property. Rather than state definitively, as Kant did a century later (1930: 165), that persons cannot be property, Locke started with the paradoxical notion that persons *are* property, their own. It becomes clear very quickly, however, that the universal rhetoric of his statements about 'every Man' does not actually apply to all men or to women. Locke challenged certain social hierarchies, in particular those which gave absolute political power to the monarch and aristocracy. At the same time, he explicitly reasserted the hierarchies of class and gender, and strengthened the (at that time) less entrenched racial and cultural distinctions: thus, one key critical position concerning his work focuses upon the limited scope of his description of human liberty. As Barbara Arneil illustrates in detail, despite its critique of feudal status, Locke's world-view remained essentially hierarchical. This hierarchy was drawn in relation to property, the public/private distinction, and according to race, class and gender:[1]

> His theory seems to imply that free male citizens have ultimate authority, but . . . their wives have similar authority within marriage over their children, servants and slaves . . ., servants have rights over their own lives and wages . . . but not their labour; 'Indians', who should not be enslaved into the domestic sphere of another, have rights over basic subsistence . . . but not over property in land . . . and, finally, African slaves have no rights of property whatsoever and are to be fully submerged in the private sphere . . . It is crucial to note that in each of the last three categories (servant, Amerindian, African slave), there are both men and women, whose status in relation to property far outweighs the differences between them based on gender.
>
> (Arneil 2001: 41)

Thus, despite the principle that every man owns himself, Locke nonetheless assumed the legitimacy of slavery, and of other class distinctions. 'Man' was free from domination in the state of nature, and was free under political rule from all domination except that which had been established by consent: slavery, however, was the consequence of a third condition – the state of war – and slaves were essentially the legitimate spoils of lawful conquest (Locke 1988: 284). In other words, Locke's self-owning man was basically the free capitalist accumulator: not his wife, his male or female servants and agricultural labourers, and much less his slaves. Outside the household the 'Indians' in the state of nature were free to appropriate, but only under the conditions set by natural law: that is, without money they could not accumulate property, but only appropriate as much as they could productively use.

On the one hand, law has obviously passed beyond these social distinctions. Slavery has been abolished in law if not in practice, wives have been freed from the legal incapacities which once subjected them to their husbands, and Indigenous people have a formal equality with the non-Indigenous. The status of those household servants who have survived the social transitions of the past several hundred years is the more dignified one of 'employee', and breaking an employment contract is no longer a criminal offence. Nonetheless, the old Lockean hierarchies remain embedded in the symbolism and the broad cultural resonance of property: distinctions of gender, race, and class still inflect what it means to be a person and a proprietor, and persons as proprietors remain one norm of contemporary legal and political discourse. In other words, the meaning of property and the meaning of the person remain intermingled in a network of racial, class and gender associations.

For instance, in Chapter 2 I considered some of the symbolic implications of this picture of the person as an essentially self-enclosed, or as Nedelsky puts it, 'bounded' entity (Nedelsky 1990; cf. Naffine 1997 and 1998). In particular, I noted the strong resonance of the self-proprietor with the image of the white, Western, propertied male: on the level of representation, the self-possessed person connotes membership of a specific culture, class and gender. Common law history also shows that legal personality has been associated with the ability to own, and with the right of physical self-possession. Thus women, whose bodies were controlled by fathers and husbands, and who could not own property in their own right (at least when married), were not 'persons'. Similarly, as I will explain shortly, ownership or custodianship which was not based on the liberal model of individual and private ownership, was often not recognised as ownership at all, and nor were the holders of such property viewed as persons.[2]

A first critical response to Locke's self-owning person is therefore that the principle is not extended to all. Locke clearly thought it was reasonable to exclude certain classes of people, in fact most people, from the liberty and self-governance which goes along with self-ownership. From a modern perspective these exclusions are easily dismissed as based upon on a narrow or only partially enlightened understanding of human relationships and capacities (Parekh 1995). Indeed, the notion that people naturally own themselves and have a moral right to the fruits of their own labour, has for centuries provided an immensely powerful argument for many emancipatory projects. Marx insisted that the worker 'must be the untrammelled owner of his capacity for labour' who can sell it for a limited term only, 'for if he were to sell it rump and stump, once for all, he would be selling himself, converting himself from a free man into a slave' (Marx 1947: 146).[3] Feminists have also used the idea extensively in campaigning for women's bodily self-determination including reproductive freedoms.

Even when equalised and modernised, however, the image of

self-ownership contains implicit social hierarchies, leading to a second critical response relating to the 'natural' status of the self-owning person. Locke's justification of original acquisition was based on the thought that each person/man *begins* by owning himself. This principle is a part of the natural law according to Locke: the person does not acquire himself and nor is self-possession the consequence of a political or legal process. The self is a pre-social, pre-legal, and pre-political entity (cf. Thomas 2003: 38). Ownership of the self is a correspondingly natural and pre-social principle. Where the positivist Bentham said that 'property and law are born together and die together' (Bentham 1931:113), Locke's natural law theory essentially states that property and the *self* are born together and die together. Locke's derivation of private property from a subject existing in the state of nature presupposes private property as the structure of the self, presupposes, that is, a subject who is always already constituted as owner and object. The natural self-proprietor is natural individualism: property in the self separates the self from others making one's own self an excludable resource. But on what basis can individualism be read into an allegedly 'natural' law? On what basis can it be affirmed that the individual is the creator, rather than the effect, of social and political relationships and institutions? And on what basis is property necessarily and essentially at one with individualism? To claim that a principle is 'natural' is, of course, to give it incredible political and ideological power (Žižek 1994: 11), meaning that it would be politically risky to abandon the idea of self-ownership altogether. At the same time, adopting this extreme individualism reinforces the separation of self from other: as I indicated in Chapter 2, there are alternatives to the 'bounded self' which may allow a more complex situated self to emerge as a form of connectedness with others.

Colonialism and imperialism

As it turns out, Locke's individual in the state of nature has only the power to appropriate, not accumulate: it takes money and the (implied or constructive) consent of others to amass property in the way Locke envisaged. If Locke's self-owner excluded certain classes of human being in the domestic context, it was equally if not more exploitative of Indigenous populations of emerging British colonies. Over the past two decades numbers of scholars have investigated the connection between Locke and colonialism (Lebovics 1986;

Flanagan 1989; Tully 1993; Arneil 1994; Parekh 1995; Armitage 2004). Locke's views on the relationship between labour, especially in the form of agriculture, arguably served as a powerful justification for the dispossession of first, American Indian lands, and later the lands of Indigenous peoples in other colonies, especially where the colonialists wrongly perceived that the land was essentially unused. But the connection was also reflexive, colonialism itself providing a fundamental element of Locke's work, as Lebovics has pointed out: ' "In the beginning all the World was America." [Locke] wrote . . . thereby making that vast undeveloped continent an integral part of Western political philosophy' (1986: 567). Neither the justification of colonialism nor the liberal political theory had logical precedence over the other; they were, rather, mutually constitutive. As we saw in Chapter 3, moreover, colonialism occurred in parallel with the enclosure of domestic land: both movements were associated with a discourse of improvement (Buck 2001).

The context in which Locke wrote was the scene of very intense debate about the political, moral, and economic merits of colonialism. Colonialism had some very severe critics: those who debated the political right of states to establish new sovereign territories; those who thought it involved an unjust dispossession of legitimately held land; those who thought that the economic returns did not justify the significant investment (Arneil 1994). Locke had a personal as well as a philosophical interest in the outcome of these controversies: during his life he held various offices relating to colonial administration, he was secretary to the Proprietors of Carolina, and assisted with the drafting of its Fundamental Constitutions (Arneil 1994; Armitage 2004). He also took an active interest in learning about the colonies, collecting numbers of travel books which provided some form of empirical basis for his observations about American Indian life (Arneil 1996: 22–44).

In brief, Locke's moral and political defence of colonialism is organised around two lines of argument, relating to property and political institutions. These arguments are supplemented by a pervasive Eurocentrism comprising several large and unfounded assumptions, as well as an inability to imagine the relationship between people and their resources in any way other than through the language and concepts of enclosed private property. First, as I have outlined, he argued that land and resources which were not used, or not sufficiently used, could legitimately be appropriated for the benefit of humankind. Such an appropriation was effected by labour, and did not rely on anybody's consent (1988: 289). As formulated by Locke, this argument only applied in the state of nature. It did not apply to areas of the world, such as Europe, which had gone beyond the state of nature and where property ownership was governed by positive law (ibid: 292). (As we have seen, however, a broad language of improvement was integral to the enclosure movement.) Second, he argued that the American Indians were effectively, despite what he saw as some rudimentary efforts at political society, in a *real* state of nature (his was not an imagined or hypothetical state of nature as posited by theorists such as Hobbes and Rousseau) (Tully 1993: 140–41; Parekh 1995: 86–7). In their dealings with the American Indians the colonists were bound by the laws of nature, as Locke saw them, and not by any domestic laws (cf. Locke 1967: 277, referring to the meeting of a '*Swiss* and an *Indian*, in the woods of *America*'). In their state of nature, the American Indians used land, and appropriated resources to live on, but Locke argued they had not effectively appropriated or enclosed it, referring for instance to the 'wild Indian, who knows no Inclosure and is still a tenant in common' (ibid: 287). Such statements are at the least ironic, if not deliberately misleading and manipulative, since, as Vicki Hsueh has illustrated, Locke was aware that colonists in Carolina had to learn agricultural skills from the Indigenous peoples (Hsueh 2006: 201–3). Nonetheless, the land of the Americas remained, in Locke's view, under used and was not anybody's property. Consequently, the colonialists had the right – or even the duty – to establish plantations under the natural law principles for appropriation of land and resources.

Locke lived at a time when Europeans knew relatively little about the social, political, and agricultural practices of Indigenous peoples. It is therefore easy to suggest that the treatment of this topic in the *Two Treatises* may have been the product of limited knowledge and was largely determined by the inevitably Eurocentric context within which Locke worked.[4] However, as numbers of scholars have pointed out, not all of Locke's contemporaries agreed that the lands inhabited (and cultivated) by the 'primitive' peoples of North America could be regarded as available for appropriation (Tully 1993: 147–8; Parekh 1995: 82–3). Locke had to make a positive argument in the face of opposition, as did later colonial apologists who drew on the agricultural argument in relation to other colonies such as Australia (Reynolds 1987: 168–75). The argument has been shown by subsequent scholarship to rely on an inaccurate understanding of Indigenous peoples' political and agricultural practices

(Parekh 1995; Hsueh 2006), as well as upon very limited and unimaginative perceptions of what constitutes property and political institutions. Even at the time it was formulated, the argument was subject to strong doubt on evidence-based and moral grounds. Thus, it was a strategic and political argument, even as it purported to be based upon rational and philosophical foundations.

The 'agricultural argument' for colonialism was not, of course, unique to Locke: versions of it preceded his work and new versions were put forward after his death (Tully 1993: 149–51; Flanagan 1989). In the sixteenth century Thomas More had used a version of it in *Utopia* (ibid 1989: 590). In the eighteenth century the Swiss jurist Vattel put forward an even more explicit justification of appropriation of territories in the 'new' world: 'when the Nations of Europe, which are too confined at home, come upon lands which the savages have no special need of and are making no present and continuous use of, they may lawfully take possession of them' (quoted in Flanagan 1989: 596).[5] Vattel's work in particular was used in direct justification of the colonisation of Australia (Castles 1982: 16; Reynolds 1987: 169), and gave support to the interpretation of *terra nullius* as uncultivated, rather than uninhabited, land. In practice, arguments about cultivation and improvement were deployed differently in the many different colonial contexts (Dorsett 1995; Weaver 2005). In New Zealand, the British Government recognised that the Indigenous peoples held title to the land, meaning that its exchange was theoretically governed by treaty and sales mediated by the Crown: through these mechanisms most of the country was nonetheless converted from communal Maori title to private white ownership (Weaver 2005: 93–4). In Australia, Indigenous title to land was not recognised at all until 1992, and then only really as an afterthought to the white legal system rather than on Indigenous terms: colonial policy was essentially that the land was neither owned *nor* significantly used by the Indigenous peoples.

The uses of the agricultural argument do not stop with colonialism. Expansionist capitalism continues to find new 'frontiers' capable of exploitation, often in ways which trample on the lifestyles and cultural knowledges of non-Western communities. While the genetic code of a particular group of people, their knowledge of a traditional medicine, or the biodiversity within their forests may seem a long way from Locke, such resources can be subject to essentially the same form of imperialist appropriation. In such contexts, the language of discovery, use, improvement, and the need for private property rights to ensure investment returns, frames neo-liberal interactions (Shiva 2001; Mgbeoji 2006)

HEGEL AND SOME NEW HEGELIANS

A broad Lockean view is that human beings (at least some) have a *natural* property in their persons: their labour, their abilities, and their body. For Locke, self-ownership leads to ownership of tangible things. Hegel postulated a different relationship between property and the person which did not see it as pre-existing other relationships. Rather, Hegel's person takes hold of or appropriates him or her self, but only after (or in the process of) appropriating external things. However, property is only one part of an intricate conceptual and historical process which constitutes the ethical existence of a state. Generally speaking, in Locke, the natural right of self-ownership precedes property. For Hegel, actual appropriation gives rise to personality: in a sense, persons need property to be self-fulfilled, but individual property is transcended by the more compelling demands of co-existence with others (Salter 1987). Until the late twentieth century, Hegel's work on property was not particularly influential in Anglocentric legal theory, and it certainly could not have had any practical impact in relation to English colonialism. In recent years, however, inspired no doubt by a more general interest in continental philosophy, Hegel's *Philosophy of Right* has been discovered and interpreted for the more liberal-legal context of the United States and other English-speaking legal theoretical contexts. The most well-known proponent of this reinterpretation has been the feminist theorist Margaret Radin (1993). Radin's work draws upon the property–person connection rather than the broader Hegelian system, and therefore tends to liberalise Hegel – that is, his work on property is understood as strengthening the interests of the individual against a potentially hostile social and political environment. As I will explain, Radin's aim is not to defend liberal capitalism but rather, pragmatically, to start with it as the here and now of property. Other theorists have taken a more technical and philosophical approach to Hegel's work, and have emphasised its anti-liberal, anti-natural law and communitarian character (Salter 1987; Carlson 2000; Schroeder 1994b). However, this type of work seems to have less direct practical impact than Radin's (see Schnably 1993: 349 fn 10 for a summary of some of these applications).

Appropriating the self

To begin with, an overview of Hegel's analysis of property as it appears in *The Philosophy of Right* is necessary. Having said that, it is extremely difficult to provide anything like an 'overview' of Hegel's thoughts on property. This is for two reasons. First, Hegel's theory of property, while in one sense occupying less than 20 pages of the *Philosophy of Right*, is only one small element of an extensive political theory. Focusing only upon these pages reduces the question of property to the relationship between persons and things, whereas (more so than with Locke) property for Hegel is about the system of right and positive law as a whole. It does not precede law, but nor is it simply an arbitrary construct of positive law. Second, there are undoubtedly problems with the Hegelian language which is highly abstract and individual. As far as possible, I will attempt to render the core ideas in plain English, though undoubtedly some of the nuances will be lost in doing so.

As part of the philosophy of right, property for Hegel is neither a concept nor an actual thing, but part of a process in which the concept and the actuality come together as an Idea (Hegel 1952, §1) The Idea is not, as might be assumed, a merely abstract notion but must be 'actualised' or brought into being (Hegel 1975: §142). There are initially three elements to the actualisation of property and the concurrent formation of the person. These relate to (1) the immediate abstract person, who (2) puts him or her self into the external world, and (3) appropriates things as property, thereby resolving the contradiction between self and other which arises in (2). These three steps or 'moments' provide a useful study in Hegel's broader method of 'speculative reason' which consists generally of the stage of immediacy or the self-same; the stage of division and contradiction; and the stage of sublation or resolution. However, to focus only upon these three steps in the process neglects the fact that the dialectic does not stop at the end of this first stage of 'abstract right', but continues until it reaches what Hegel regards as the ethical totality – the State. Even in the initial stages of *The Philosophy of Right*, property does not rest with its subjective construction: it is arguably the recognition of the person as an owner by others in contract which consolidates and makes 'objective' the claimed property right.[6] I will now explain all of this in more detail.

To begin with, the subject is a free will, an abstract entity who has 'no property and no "properties" ' (Carlson 2000: 1380). Such a self is only internal, a 'self-conscious but otherwise contentless and simple relation of itself to itself in its individuality' (Hegel 1952: §34). This is not a stage in human development, but rather a 'moment' in self-construction, or one part of ourselves which is absolutely internal and not related to the external world.

Second, Hegel postulated that in order to actualise or realise one's personality it was necessary to project one's will into the external world: 'A person must translate his freedom into an external sphere in order to exist as Idea' (Hegel 1952: §41). The externality which is opposed to the abstract self is the world of 'things' which is opposed to the person: a thing does not have rights and is not an 'end in itself' (ibid: §44), meaning that it 'derives its destiny and soul' from a person's will (ibid: §44). Things might be tangible objects, but they can also be a person's own skills, wisdom, and abilities which may be 'expressed', that is, externalised, and subsequently made the subject of a contract (ibid: §43). Third, the externalised will is reappropriated in the form of property. If a person has occupancy or possession of something, that thing becomes property[7] by virtue of the fact that the person's will is projected into the thing, and taken back into the self. This is a difficult point to comprehend, so here is another attempt to explain it. I identify myself in the blue pot on my desk – it is my 'other', but I project my will into it and bring this (with the pot) back into my self. In so doing, I grasp it for my own, and see my objectified will in it. This action constitutes (note, this is different from 'justifies') my property in the pot, and it also constitutes myself because I have formed a relationship with the other (that is, at this point, the external world of things). I become an actual person by relating to myself through the external world. There are many possible issues and problems which can be raised here, but in the interests of brevity, I will not explore them.[8]

However, the constitutions of property and the person do not rest with this self-motivated appropriation of external things. Rather, it gives rise to a further process of contradiction and resolution in contract. Hegel argues that the person relates to other people through contract. All the while the person's will is in an object which they think of as their own, this may come into conflict with another person who thinks that the same object belongs to them (Hegel 1952: §84; cf. Carlson 2000: 1391[9]). All the while there is just a person and a thing, there can be no rightful (or positive, in the sense of positive law) basis to property. Contract consolidates property, and makes property right and objective, because in contract the self-identified owner and another person agree: the 'property' in the thing is posited by the consent of the parties. In other words, if I try to sell you my pot and you say it is your pot or demand to know how I came by it, we have a conflict; on the other hand, if you agree to exchange it for your copy of Proudhon's *What is Property?*, we have a contract, based on the fact that we recognise each other as persons and as owners of our respective items. The persons and the property get their status as *right* by virtue of this act of mutual agreement or positing.

The differences between Hegel's account of property and Locke's are significant. Both philosophers see property as being in an integral relation to the person. However, for Locke the person already has property in him or herself before coming across any external thing or person. Appropriation occurs in the state of nature, and is justified by labour. For Hegel, the person and their property are only fully constituted through relationships with others – they are post-social, not pre-social. Most importantly, however, is the fact that the individual relationships with objects in property and with other individuals in contract are just the first stages of a process which has as its end the attainment of an ethical social totality. The individual and his or her property rights are neither the beginning nor end of the process: the interests of the individual can ultimately only be realised in conjunction with (not in competition with) the interests of the whole community (Hegel 1952: §258R). This contrasts sharply with Locke's positing of property in an alleged state of nature.

There are, of course, a number of perspectives from which to critique Hegel's thought. I do not have space (or frankly the expertise) here to go into the very extensive critiques which his work has generated. However, even without the detail, it is possible to see that Hegel's emphasis upon theorising a social totality in which a universal spirit is manifested, does not sit easily with current theoretical preferences for less totalistic understandings of social entities, a point made cogently by Fred Dallmayr:

> At a time when a theoretical premium is placed on diversity, contestation, and dispersal, the view of the state as an ethical fabric permeated by *Sittlichkeit* [ethical life] is liable to be regarded as a quaint relic of classicism – if not as the emblem of sinister totalitarian designs.
>
> (Dallmayr 1991: 321)

In addition to the rejection of metanarratives or 'grand theories' (and Hegel's theory is certainly 'grand'), scepticism has frequently been expressed by critical theorists about claims to absolutely grounded philosophy. Any 'totality' (if such a thing exists) resists theory and is characterised as much by its conceptual and empirical messiness as by its order or logic (however complicated that logic may be). For instance, Hegel's notion of a historical and logical progression expressed through dialectics as the basis for certain philosophical knowledge can seem too contrived, too contradicted by actual history, and too contingent (see generally Dallmayr 1991: 330–7). Marx and Engels, while accepting Hegel's vision of history as a process with its own inner logic, thought that his philosophy was misconceived in that it moved from ideal to real, rather than the other way around (Lukács 1971: 16–17; Engels 1968: 408–9).[10] In contrast to Hegel, Marx, *and* Engels, Nietzsche regarded it as a 'swindle' to speak of a process of world history with a determinate aim (Nietzsche 1954b: 40): 'This beautiful world history is, in Heraclitean terms, "a chaotic pile of rubbish" '(ibid: 39).

Having said that, there are, as I have indicated, some very useful and interesting aspects of Hegel's thought on property: in particular, his corrective to the Lockean notion that property and the person pre-exist social engagement, (for some) his articulation of the need for property in the attainment of personality, and his insistence that the individual and individual rights are – or ought to be – subsumed by the community.

Practical implications: 'property for personality'

For a number of reasons (both political and intellectual), Hegel's thought was almost completely abandoned by Anglocentric philosophy throughout the twentieth century. However, there has been a resurgence of interest in Hegel since the 1980s, a trend which has influenced legal theory as well as other forms of philosophy. In the first instance, Margaret Radin made use of his thought in her work about the relationship of property to personality. In reinterpreting Hegel for a modern context, Radin emphasises two types of property: that which is essential to self-construction and which is regarded as 'market inalienable' or non-commodifiable; and that which is fungible, commodifiable, and subject to commercial exchange (Radin 1993: 35–71; Radin 1996).

Radin's argument that there are types of property which ought to enjoy special protection draws upon a Hegelian insight – that persons need property in order to be respected as persons (1993: 44–8). However, according to Radin, persons do not require unlimited property, but merely those things (including their own body and capacities) which support their flourishing as a person. Such 'property for personhood' is more strongly related to human dignity and well-being than merely fungible property, meaning that it deserves greater state protection and, in some circumstances, may be 'market-inalienable' (Radin 1987).

This raises some interesting issues, such as how it is possible to determine what counts as personal property and what counts as fungible. According to Radin, there must be both a subjective and a conventional/social dimension to this issue. For instance, while some may feel that their wedding ring (to use one of Radin's examples) is property which helps to establish and define their personhood, others have no attachment, or even an antipathy, to the symbols of matrimony and would prefer to define their personhood through their vegetable patch, car, or something less tangible. In all probability, for each person who does define their personhood in relation to property there will be a unique mix of significant things.

At the same time, according to Radin there is a limit to what law can and should protect in terms of people's subjective self-constitutions: 'normal' social consensus would not support a belief that I *need* to own four aeroplanes to be a fulfilled person, and certain fetishes which are 'unhealthy' or 'insane' will – again by operation of social consensus – also be precluded from the category of property for personhood (1993: 43–4). (This does not mean complete preclusion from the category of property – such items would still be regarded as fungible property.) Thus, the subjective perception of what is important for the self is ultimately limited by social convention. On the other hand, who is really to say that the person who defines themselves through their house is more 'healthy' or 'normal' than the person who fixates upon thousands of pairs of socks or shoes? What social differences are disguised by the appeal to consensus? There is an unspoken politics of normality operating at this point of Radin's argument (Schnably 1993).

'Most people', according to Radin, do define themselves through property (1993: 36). To give a common example, a house burglary is often experienced as a 'violation', that is, an attack on the person rather than simply a trespass to goods. I would not necessarily argue with the claim that many people define themselves through property, at least insofar as Radin later qualified this claim as referring to the particular cultural conditions of the liberal West: as a pragmatist, Radin 'wanted to plug into a socially constructed understanding involving connection between persons and things that matter to them' (1993: 8).[11] In characterising her view as 'pragmatic', Radin means that it is a response to an existing context, and decidedly not a universal justification for property or for some forms of property. Once we acknowledge that liberal culture does, in fact, view the person as constituted by some forms of property, the question is how to strengthen and promote individual flourishing within this context. While it might not be ideally defensible to regard persons in this way, her point is that we do, and therefore need strategies to resist the tendency towards commodification which is inherent in it. So, for instance, property for personhood might strengthen legal protection for housing tenants, since the house is often a key site for self-constitution or a 'sanctuary needed for personhood' (1993: 59). Property for personhood might redistribute the power associated with property so that each person is better able to fulfil their personal needs. It potentially recognises and challenges the fact that one person's accumulation of wealth can be at the expense of another's ability to live a dignified life. Another strategic purpose for constructing this argument is to counteract the 'universal commodification' approach, especially associated with neo-liberal economics, which would make *all* human existence available to the market (1987). The law and economics writer Richard Posner is one well-known theorist who would reduce many if not all human capacities and relationships to an economic model. Posner's human market extends to sexual relationships or perhaps more correctly sexual 'exchanges' (Posner 1992), babies (Landes and Posner 1978) and, more recently and more moderately, law clerks (Avery et al. 2001). The worthwhile, indeed necessary, purpose behind Radin's argument is to protect the person from the most extreme market forces: one feminist outcome specifically addressed by Radin is legally restricting the many ways in which women and women's bodies can be commodified.

There are several key areas for the critique of Radin's work (see generally Schnably 1993; Davies and Naffine 2001: 6–9). First, she arguably relies too heavily on a notion of personal identity which is derived from one's attachment to objects rather than our connections with other subjects (Schroeder 1994b). Does such a perspective

undervalue relationships and, moreover, reinforce the liberal individualist norm of autonomy and separation from others? Second,
Radin's appeal to social convention or normality in determining the
nature of property for personhood raises issues about who determines the 'normal'. As I have said, the idea of a social 'normality' is
often very problematic and reinforces already powerful conventions,
while repressing others which may be just as ethically defensible. As
Stephen Schnably argues in his excellent critique of Radin (1993), a
personhood object such as the home is not politically innocent but
rather contestable and, in fact, contested by dissidents, by marginal-
ised groups, and by those who wish to construct alternative narratives for themselves. The home is the barrier separating public from
private – often to the detriment of women. In the suburban landscape homes exist within communities, which enforce racial and
class divisions (Schnably 1993: 365–6). And the very ideal of the
home as essential to the individual person or nuclear family may
itself be related to homelessness by placing a value and scarcity upon
a certain type of home (rather than, for instance, encouraging more
communal living) (cf. Schnably 1993: 375–9). If the home is an
extended part of the self, then its wider meanings – gendered, raced
and otherwise divisive – also become part of one's identity. Or at
least, uncritical acceptance of the property for personhood paradigm masks the contestable meanings of key personality constitu-
ents and strengthens the powerful discourses of the normal. This is
also evident in relation to consumer culture, in which Schnably says
'all commodities have implications for personhood: the category of
"fungible" property is an empty one' (1993: 391). Finally, while persons may indeed construct themselves through property, is acknowledging this through law – rather than challenging it – a productive
strategy? Would it be preferable to think of our relationship with the
external world not through the lens of property which connotes
exclusion, power and control of external things, but through some
other means? Should the law reinforce a cultural tendency which is
divisive and, in Marx's terminology, alienating for the self?

Hegelian–Lacanian intersections

If Hegel on property and abstract right is challenging to read, then
Jeanne Schroeder's Hegelian–Lacanian reading of property theory
is even more challenging. Classical German philosophy is *nearly*
always difficult, structuralist French psychoanalysis always so. I do

not intend (partly because of its intricacy) to explain the theory in detail, merely highlight several of the connections between property and psychoanalysis which Schroeder explores.

Both Hegel and Radin argued that relationship to the external world through property is an integral moment in self-construction. There is no absolute distinction between the person and the external world because what begins as 'external' becomes part of the person, part of their identity. Private ownership – taking hold of and controlling objects to the exclusion of others – is the mechanism for this relationship. Being a person is connected to having property, but in 'having' property the person is also property – their own. The self is split between having and being property. The Hegelian process refers rather broadly to identity or personality formation, without specifying exactly what is being formed and why people feel the need to relate to objects in this way. Schroeder's approach, which combines Hegelian theory with the psychoanalysis of Jacques Lacan, tries to go deeper into the psychic dimensions of property as constitutive of self.

One significant aspect of self-constitution emphasised by psychoanalytical theorists is the construction of gender, which, as we have seen, often implicates a property metaphor. The nineteenth-century French anarchist Pierre-Joseph Proudhon is famous for saying that 'property is theft' (Proudhon 1994: 13). He is less well known for describing the difference between possession and property thus: 'a lover is a possessor, a husband a proprietor' (ibid: 36). Putting the two propositions together, can we deduce that a husband is also a thief, bringing us right up to the 1980s and Catharine MacKinnon, who not quite as famously but just as powerfully said '[s]exuality is to feminism what work is to Marxism: that which is most one's own, yet most taken away' (MacKinnon 1982: 515). Schroeder's analysis is situated within the long and distinguished feminist tradition (of which MacKinnon is one part) which highlights and attacks the literal and figural commodification of women. Women are propertised in the economy of male ownership and property is feminised, as in the boat or car which is referred to as 'she'. In this heterosexual economy, property and women are both objects of desire and exchange. However, this economy does not simply degrade and objectify women, it *constitutes* gender: thus, the objectification and exchange of women is the basis upon which the construction of male subjectivity proceeds.

Things become a bit more contentious when the psychoanalytical dimension is brought in. 'Contentious' for two reasons: first, what looks like a symbolic identification of women with a male body-part; and second, the fixed nature of gender as a dualism. Schroeder's argument is that property and 'Woman' serve the same purpose in the construction of masculine subjectivity. She says:

> They are both types of the 'Phallus' in the sense of the psycho-analytic term for the object of desire. Both property, according to Hegelian philosophy, and the Feminine, according to Lacanian psychoanalysis, are fictions we write to serve as the defining external objects enabling us to constitute ourselves as acting subjects. By serving as objects of exchange between subjects, property and the Feminine simultaneously enable subjects to recognize other humans as individual subjects – they enable us to desire and to be desired.
>
> (Schroeder 1995: 816)

In psychoanalytical thought the 'phallus' is not actually a male body part, but a constitutive signifier 'for the cultural privileges and positive values which define male subjectivity within patriarchal society, but from which the female subject remains isolated' (Silverman 1983: 183).[12] Schroeder suggests that woman and property both take on this role as that object of desire which is necessary for the constitution of the male subject. (The question remains, of course, as to why the 'phallus' is the term for this signifier, and what its relationship is to the male body, but I cannot get into that here: see Silverman 1983: 184.)

According to Schroeder there is not only an *analogy* between women and property. It is rather that they perform the same symbolic function in defining and mediating masculine subjectivity:

> When men speak of possessing a woman in sexual intercourse, they do not make an analogy to the possession of real property as the right to enter and the power to prevent others from entering. The two are not merely similar; they are psychoanalytically identical.
>
> (Schroeder 1994a: 255)

Thus Schroeder's characterisation of the relationship between women and property emphasises their symbolic function. Both are objects of desire to be exclusively possessed in a masculine economy. Although I remain unconvinced of the necessity of the psychoanalytical framework in reaching this understanding, and although I am wary of the

potential normalisation of women's lack of subjectivity in psychoanalytical thought, it does represent a descriptive tool which – if not
taken literally – may be of some value.

Although her analysis is more explicitly psychoanalytical than
most, Schroeder is only one of many critical theorists to notice a
parallel between the function of property as a means of exchange
and communication between men, and the role of women as objects
of mediation. The critical anthropologist Levi-Strauss, for instance,
described the socio-economic function of women as objects of
exchange between men, thereby constituting the means of communication and contract between men (Levi-Strauss 1969). In different
ways, a number of feminists such as Pateman, Irigaray, and Wittig
(who explicitly compares women as a class to the feudal class of
serfs) have analysed and critiqued the ownership paradigm of heterosexual relations (Pateman 1988; Irigaray 1985; Wittig 1992).[13]
These feminist critiques attack both the symbolic or metaphorical
construction of heterosexual relations through the concept of property, and also the material conditions of heterosexual existence,
which include the actual commodification of women in sexual and
other marketplaces – through prostitution, pornography, surrogacy,
trafficking, and so forth.

While acknowledging that 'Lacan's theory is virulently misogynist'
(Schroeder, 1994a: 318), like Irigaray, Schroeder appears to accept
Lacan's fundamental proposition that there is a *necessary* structural
difference between the masculine and the feminine which constitutes
the symbolic order. Therefore the feminist strategy for Schroeder, as
for the European 'sexual difference' feminists, is to *reconfigure* the
relationship between masculine and feminine, not to envisage or
work towards a transgression of the structural dichotomy in sexual
symbolism. Schroeder's feminist strategy involves 'the rewriting of
the myth of the Feminine as an active mediatrix' which 'requires
the creation of feminine subjectivity' (Schroeder 1994a: 318; cf.
Schroeder 1994b: 165–71). Like Irigaray, Schroeder does not reject
the basic sexual dichotomy, but argues instead that *within* our category it is possible for women to invent a subjectivity, to be active, not
passive or invisible, while fulfilling the seemingly necessary function
of object-ness or mediation.

Schroeder's analysis relies upon both Hegel's and Lacan's respective articulations of the roles of property and Woman. Men need
women/property to constitute themselves as subjects relating to
each other. If these relationships are seen as contestable cultural

productions, rather than ontological necessities, the analysis is quite compelling and may even be said to reveal a certain complicity between capitalism and patriarchy. However, while emphasising throughout that Lacanian theory is fundamentally a description of culturally entrenched psychic fantasies which could be otherwise, Schroeder still appears to universalise sexual difference, while accepting Hegel's argument that property is a necessary and constitutive feature of freedom and full personality. On the other hand, both the sexual dichotomy and the concept of the person who achieves freedom through property can equally be regarded as produced and subject to challenge.

Psychoanalysis prompts several possibly naive, but persistent, questions: if the object of property is analogous to the Feminine as a sort of universalised object of desire, what happens when it is (heterosexual, bisexual or lesbian) women who are doing the desiring? Who is the subject who needs the feminine to constitute itself as a subject? Why must the mediating role be characterised as 'feminine', and why is it necessary to adopt such a clearly differentiated gender configuration? There are undoubtedly answers to these questions to be found within psychoanalysis, but the point is also a political one. While I certainly accept the feminist argument that female identity is a politically charged category which makes activism and change possible, I regard its use as a strategic necessity, not an ontological one which would lock us into a sexual difference per se.

HAVING AND BEING

There is something inscrutable about the relationship between property and the person. In one sense, the relationship of property and the person is just about lines of demarcation between objects and subjects – who counts as a person and what counts as property. Sometimes, as I explained in Chapter 3, entities have moved in and out of these categories (slaves, women, children, animals), illustrating the politically, socially and legally constituted nature of the demarcation. From this angle, the issue is about whether you *have* property or *are* property. However, as we have seen in this chapter, there is also a more immanent ontological angle to the issue – for the philosophers, the property–person nexus is also about who we are, how we become, how we relate. And beyond the abstract justifications and descriptions, the property–person nexus is strongly cultural – it is about how we are situated as sexed beings, how we are situated racially, how power is distributed symbolically and actually in our political economies. All of these demarcations and associations are highly contestable, though driven by what might be termed a 'politics of the proper'[14] where our proper person, our property, and our properties are all bound together in a network of meanings. Thus for Hegel and Locke, though the mechanism, the end point, and the process differed, persons were still constituted through some relation with property, and through their ability to own themselves. While there are certainly counter-stories within Western philosophy (e.g. Kant), I think it is evident from this chapter and from Chapter 2 that property and the person are powerfully related in key narratives of Western culture. To finalise this chapter, I would like to consider whether the dichotomy between having and being and the sexual symbolism connected with property can be disrupted or thought differently.

As we have seen, classical notions of the person demand that a person who is able to own property is not herself or himself property (except possibly their own), whereas the human being who is owned is not a person. The modern resistance to any relationship which would overtly commodify a person owes its force to this logic. One may either *have* property or *be* property. There is also tension in this distinction when it is applied to the concept of self-ownership, because this implies that one simultaneously is and owns oneself. Having and being oneself defines the person and sets an exclusion zone around the person. Several categories of human being who are not culturally regarded as self-owners then become both legally and socially/symbolically open to objectification. Critical thought offers several distinct possibilities for counteracting this, some of which have already been outlined at the end of Chapter 2. The issue I want to address here is whether it is possible to rethink the dichotomies of having/being; subject/object; masculine/feminine; and ultimately owner/owned.[15]

Some theorists have suggested that a breakdown or subversion of the subject/object distinction will be emancipatory in our ethical relationships (Laclau 1996: 1), and it seems to me that one aspect of this is a deconstruction of the boundaries between having and being. Patricia Williams has suggested, for example, that rights including the right to private property ought to be given away freely in an effort to reformulate the individuation of subjects set apart from objects 'so that we may say not that we own gold, but that a luminous golden spirit owns us' (Williams 1987: 401). The tantalising thought here is that being does not have to be understood as a natural condition or a reflection of our individual efforts at appropriation, but rather may be regarded as a gift in process – connecting the self in perpetuity to the other, and implying a constant effort at reconciliation, rather than domination.

Contemporary critical theorists have denaturalised the subject (that is, *all* subjects, not just those who are 'different' from the white masculine norm), seeing it as the effect of multiple and complex systems of meaning, rather than a self-defined unit. Signifiers such as the gender markers 'masculine' and 'feminine' may become detached from their normalised positions. Queer theory and some types of feminism emphasise this fluidity of gender in an effort to subvert social normality, to see it differently. Insofar as the queer is concerned to accentuate the *improper* generally, and possibly the improper potential of every person, one important aspect of a queer approach is critique of this propriety, and of property symbolism tied to sex (see, for example, Butler 1993: 62, 88). Thus, there is no need to insist on a fixed gender distinction, much less the association of gender with a position as subject or object of property/desire. These relationships are certainly resilient cultural constructions, but are all open to reinvention.

This may all appear to be rather abstract: the central point is that an alternative reading of the relationship between having and being might be seen as posing a challenge to the distinction between person and property – not only to its gendered associations, but also to the structure of property as a grant of personal sovereignty. On the practical level, it is possible to understand the legal relationship between personal rights and property as – in some elementary sense – involving a coming together of self and other (as implied, for instance, in Hegel), rather than simple domination of the other by the owner. For instance, increasing recognition that property carries both rights and responsibilities (Raff 1998; Singer 2000; cf. Eleftheriadis 1996: 40–41) – we own the object, but it also owns us, in that it limits our behaviour – may in fact signal some fundamental movement away from the modern liberal view of the proprietor as sovereign. If my ownership is limited by the interests of others, then the property is a relationship *between* us, not merely an extension of my personality.

The ambivalence in the having/being distinction in property may also be expressed as the non-reducibility of personal identity to exclusive self-ownership. As I indicated earlier, self-ownership, self-possession, self-identity are all models which attempt to collapse identity into itself, but which inevitably rely upon a fragmented person, and a person who at once is, and has possession of, themselves. Current thinking about identity has taken the notion of fragmentation much further: personal identity is not an essence which can in any simple sense own even another aspect of itself, but is rather an effect of cultural and linguistic processes of construction, as well as a metaphysics which masks these processes and creates a fiction of unity. Finally, therefore, I want to ask, if the self is not self-limited or self-possessed, what becomes of ownership of external objects? Does recognition of the fragmented person provide some potential for a different view of property?

In liberal thought it is essentially the *self*-referential nature of the individual which provides the connection between the person and the (private) property. It is because the person is regarded as committed essentially to their own identity, and that that identity is primarily self-contained and self-constructing, that these connections can even arise on the different levels in which I have just outlined them (Zucker 1993: 88). An other-referential self, or, the concept of a person for whom subjectivity including sexuality is a secondary effect of social relationships, cannot sustain in the same way the connection with private property. Where the other is not simply the objectified outside of the self which may be appropriated and reduced, but rather a potentially positive, respected and celebrated element of the context within which a subject is created, the concept of private property as the means of mediation between self-contained persons is no longer sustainable.

If my relationship to myself is not simply one of self-referentiality, or self-ownership, then I can hardly be said to have a unidirectional, determining, sovereign relationship to anything external which I am said to own. Indeed, one function of private property has been to shore up the ideology of individualism by creating and protecting selves separated along proprietorial lines, but private property itself relies upon this myth of the separate person. If identity is not just personal identity which we each own individually but an identity which is owned and developed in common with others, then it cannot provide a general basis for purely private ownership, because the self always *owes* its own identity to the community. Ordinarily this debt of the person is written off or erased in the name of the individual, and, in particular, in the name of the self-owning masculine individual: rediscovering it potentially leads to a notion of property which is neither sovereign, limited, nor entirely private.

Envisaging such a conception of property is no easy task, because within this Western, Anglo-American legal culture there is no language that transcends the division of subject and object, of separated self and other, or of male and female. Jennifer Nedelsky captures the problem by saying that we 'will need a new vocabulary, new metaphors to invoke if we are not to be sucked back into the forms we are resisting even as we argue against them' (Nedelsky 1990: 181). However, perhaps new forms may be drawn out of the old: by emphasising that which – *within* the complex web of philosophical, legal and social understandings of property – appears to pose a challenge to the traditionally rigid and oppositional rhetoric of property, new approaches will gradually emerge.

CONCLUSION

The distinction between having and being which has been so important to the person–property distinction and its expression in the subject-male/object-female hierarchy is unsustainable philosophically, and like these other distinctions, is susceptible to deconstruction. This is most immediately evident in the very notion of self-ownership which conflates having and being property, but also flows from recognition of the social nature of the person. Appreciation of the contextual and dynamic character of persons, rather than their fixity and stability as simple self-owners, opens up the concept of property for reconsideration, as well as the positioning of persons in the sexual economy. If persons are never fully private or individuated entities, then the justification for private ownership which relies upon property in the person begins to look decidedly shaky.

Finally, I would not go so far as to say that the future of property is collective or communal, but only that it is not simply private or exclusive (Freyfogle 2006). I have indicated at numerous points that property can be seen as a complex of relations, rather than a simple 'despotic dominion' over a thing. As Kevin Gray has argued, private property is not 'truly private' because it is regulated and protected by the state, and because it confers a very public power over others (Gray 1991: 304). Nor is the person ever 'truly private': continuing to rethink the question of the relationship between the person and the community with a focus on property must lead to a new understanding of property as an institution. The next chapter will introduce some of the possibilities for such an altered understanding of property.

Notes

1 This is Arneil's summary of a detailed analysis of Locke's writings regarding status. It is impossible to do justice to that analysis here. The passage quoted includes a large number of explanations in parentheses which have been omitted.

2 The infamous *terra nullius* doctrine, accepted by Australian law until 1992, asserted that Australia was settled, rather than conquered. This could only be the case if Australia was regarded as uninhabited. The case which overturned the doctrine of *terra nullius* in its application to Australia was *Mabo v Queensland* (No 2) (1992) 175 Commonwealth Law Reports 1.

3 And indeed, as Marx mentions in a footnote, the practice of debt-bondage or peonage effectively reinstitutes slavery: this involves a person repaying their debts with their labour, usually at a very low rate, meaning that there is no definite end to the period of 'employment'. In some cases, the debt is also passed down through the generations, meaning that people are born into servitude.

4 As I see it, Eurocentrism is not in itself the problem, since every scholar works within a cultural context: the problem is unreflective Eurocentrism in judging non-European societies. This has hardly been eliminated from scholarship.

5 As Flanagan points out, Vattel's justification of colonialism was based upon the rights of nations, rather than the rights and nature of persons: the focus upon individual right is perhaps what has made Locke's theory such a powerful rhetorical force for appropriation.

6 My summary is necessarily very brief. For a fuller and very clear explanation see Carlson 2000.

7 'Property' in a philosophical rather than a legal sense.

8 For instance, can I 'abandon' my property while retaining possession of it – what if I forget that I own a blue pot (see ibid: §62)? Is property necessarily limited to what one can meaningfully put one's will into?

9 While I agree with Carlson's central point that contract is necessary for property, and not just the consequence of property, I am not entirely convinced that it is the 'foundation' of property or that '[u]ntil contract, the free self's claim to property was criminal because it denied right to any other free self' (Carlson 2000: 1391). I am more comfortable with the idea that until contract, property is neither right nor wrong, because it is not posited by consent. It is just a subjective claim. Having said that, I do rely on the gist of Carlson's exposition, especially as it relates to the role of contract.

10 For instance Engels wrote: 'To [Hegel] the thoughts in his brain were not the more or less abstract pictures of actual things and processes, but,

conversely, things and their evolution were only the realised pictures of the "Idea", existing somewhere from eternity before the world was. This way of thinking turned everything upside down, and completely reversed the actual connection of things in the world. Correctly and ingeniously as many individual groups of facts were grasped by Hegel, yet, for the reasons just given, there is much that is botched, artificial, laboured, in a word, wrong in point of detail' (Engels 1968: 408).

11 The chapter of *Reinterpreting Property* which deals with 'Property and Personhood' was originally published as an article by Radin in the early 1980s. The Introduction to the book qualifies and explains some of the earlier positions. While both pieces therefore have the same publication date, it is clear that there was a development of her views in the 11 years between the Introduction and Chapter 1.

12 Silverman actually describes this as the second of two meanings given by Lacan to the phallus: the first relates to that which is lost when a subject enters into the symbolic order. Basically, in learning language the subject loses something and this loss is represented by the phallus (1983: 183–4).

13 Wittig's concern is, of course, somewhat different from that of Irigaray's and Pateman's, who have each written of a sexual contract between men, which constitutes social and political relationships. Wittig's concern has been to highlight the *heterosexual* nature of the contract: that is, to indicate that it structures the world of sexual relationships *as* heterosexual.

14 I.e. in addition to Derrida's 'metaphysics of the proper'.

15 The following thoughts were originally developed in a longer and more complex form in relation to queer theory: Davies 1999. In order to simplify matters, I have contracted the argument here, but this should not be taken to imply that I have rejected its queer dimension.

Chapter 5

Horizons

The philosophers have only *interpreted* the world, in various ways; the point, however, is to *change* it.

(Marx 1845: XI)

INTRODUCTION

So far, this book has considered what might be seen by some to be a frustratingly narrow range of critical approaches to property. Each chapter has emphasised a particular aspect of property – meanings, histories, and theories – and attempted to draw from this basis some key critical thoughts or approaches. Taking a broadly defined idea of critique so that it refers equally to immanent and social critiques, the book has ranged over feminism, postmodernism, postcolonialism, critiques of race, and other approaches. But the focus has been, fairly unwaveringly, on the notion of property as a legal, political, and cultural construct: despite the critique, I have rarely considered views which provide alternatives to private property or which try to envision it in a more inclusive way.

Why is it necessary or at least productive to think about alternatives to contemporary notions of private property? Hopefully, a number of reasons for the need to think of property differently have become evident throughout this book. Here is a summary of some of these reasons. (1) Strong social and popular ideas of property associate it with rightful individual control over things to the exclusion of all non-owners. This view is counteracted by the need for a more socially and environmentally responsive relationship with resources. (2) The technical notion that property consists of a 'disaggregated' bundle of rights has the potential to reduce every right or relationship to property, and may serve to facilitate new forms of commodification which go beyond mere thing-ownership. (3) Justifications for property based on the moral imperative to improve upon nature or make the most of God-given resources have been implicated in colonialism and new forms of imperialism. (4) Private property coupled with a profit-imperative can result in the enclosure of common and public forms of ownership. (5) The incommensurability of Western forms of property with non-Western ideas of ownership has facilitated various forms of cultural appropriation. (6) Property is a defining metaphor for a particular kind of self (bounded, individual, atomistic) which is gendered, raced and otherwise exclusive. (7) Property is strongly implicated in various forms of social exclusion, both symbolic and material. (8) Despite the liberal rhetoric of equality, property ownership, especially in very concentrated forms (for instance in large corporations), undermines the distinction between private and public power: private property is itself a form of public power. These criticisms or problems do not necessarily lead to the view that private property ought to be abandoned: it is arguably not private property which is the source of these problems, but rather the expression of private property in a particular economic, cultural and political context.

In this chapter, therefore, my aim is to provide a sense of what might lie beyond the dominant idea of private property. In a sense, the answer is easy – nothing lies beyond, since in the (Western, liberal) present, our laws, our political communities, our lives, are very much shaped by the presence, the boundaries and the weight of property. It is literally not possible to live without it and, perhaps worse, it is difficult to define oneself without reference to its metaphorical resonances – the 'I' as a self-determining and bounded entity, different from and exclusive of 'you', the other. Indeed, as we have seen, this metaphorical strength of property can be tactically valuable – for instance, when defending the concept of bodily autonomy and the right to individual self-determination.

However, as feminist theorists have often pointed out, there comes a time for theory to suspend critique and enjoy a 'utopian moment'. Any theory which wants to make some difference, for instance, by challenging a distribution of power or helping to reallocate social values, must at some point confront the future: it must consider what is desirable and possible. Wendy Brown, for instance, puts it like this:

If we underscore only what we take to be sexist and materialist

constraints and we fail to practice living beyond these constraints in the present, we fail to build a bridge to another world
with our feminist knowledge projects and everyday practices. At
best, we leave the emancipation of gender, or from gender, to
imagined better days. But if we do not strain in this moment
toward another world, and especially toward pleasure and freedom, we live as if these constraints were total, which means that
invention and possibility is not part of our politics.

(Brown 2003: 367)

Similarly, while it may be difficult to look beyond property, since it
seems to fill up so much of the available practical and intellectual
space, it is nonetheless important to think about ways in which property and the politics of property can be resisted, challenged, or
reconceptualised. This need arises from the inherent limitations of
the concept in its own cultural context, that of the (neo)liberal West,
and also from the exploitation which so often occurs when it is
transposed unthinkingly into other cultural contexts.

For the purposes of this chapter, I would like to outline four
modes of disrupting and possibly changing the contemporary meanings and distributions of property. These are not separate intellectual
or activist movements, but simply a taxonomy which I have adopted
for the purposes of this chapter. In no sense are the categories pure,
self-contained, or mutually exclusive: rather each just names a theme
or general approach which is ordinarily combined with other strategies. Briefly, the four modes are as follows:

- oppositional: strategies which counteract or negate private
  property and/or global consumer culture, without necessarily
  offering any alternative vision;
- reflexive: efforts to turn private property against itself, and using
  private property to challenge the distributions of power and
  goods associated with dominant conceptions of property;
- alternative: constructing different concepts of property, and/or
  rediscovering non-private forms of ownership from Western legal
  history;
- utopian and experimental: using philosophical methods to envisage and live new legal and political structures.

Before going into details about any of these strategies, several
important introductory points need to be made. First, it is rare to

find anyone who advocates the *total* abolition of private property: even those anarchists and communists who have most strongly argued against the institution of private property have been motivated primarily by unequal distributions of property and of the social and political power it brings. Where property can be dissociated from these distributional consequences, and certainly in relation to subsistence requirements and non-exploitative ownership regimes, there is much less resistance. Resistance to private property is not (usually) to personal property, at least in its relatively modest form, but rather to ownership of resources which (it is argued) ought not to be owned privately at all; such resources could be the means of capitalist production, land, natural resources, national infrastructure, items of cultural and social value, and so forth. Obviously, there are both legal and illegal methods of resisting or challenging property. Many people who commit legal wrongs against property do not do so consciously in order to disrupt foundational politico-social institutions. Some, however, do and it is important to think about the ways in which such breaches can lead to either a real challenge to property, or a political reaction which may strengthen it.

Second, much contemporary activism and debate does not necessarily concern a rejection of private property as such, but is rather concerned with the consequences of contemporary capitalism, neo-liberalism, neo-colonialism, corporate globalisation, and consumerism. For instance, the 'Buy Nothing' campaign does not reject property; it rejects excessive consumerism. Nonetheless, I consider a few examples of such campaigns here, because they represent a challenge to some of the extended meanings and expressions of private property in advanced capitalist contexts.

Third, considered broadly, forms of scholarship and activism which challenge property in some fundamental way are actually very diverse and numerous. It would be quite impossible in a short space to offer any kind of comprehensive analysis or even a good solid overview of these matters. As usual, the thoughts I offer here are partial and selective, though I have tried to indicate something of the range of different approaches and possibilities. Undoubtedly there are many other interesting angles on this.

OPPOSITIONAL TACTICS

A first option for challenging dominant ideas about property, and in particular its extensively privatised and market-driven form, is oppositional. Much of the activism and commentary which rejects private property or simply critiques it (like the greater part of this book) does not offer any particular alternative – it simply represents a negative dimension to property and property discourse. In one sense, a negative or rejective consciousness about private property is rather ordinary, especially when this takes the form of some illegal act. Theft and squatting, after all, are common enough methods of negating tangible property. And in relation to certain forms of intangible property, there seem to be few legal (and even fewer moral) disincentives to infringement: illicit sharing, copying, or distribution of music, movies, and other electronically available resources is clearly widespread.[1] A generalisation about transgressions of both tangible and intangible property is that they can be indeterminate on several levels. They can be driven by a pro- or anti-property agenda (or by simple need), and can result in a strengthening or a dilution of traditional property rights.[2]

For instance, widespread copyright infringement, particularly of music, is made possible by 'peer-to-peer' (P2P) file sharing over the internet, a practice underpinned by widely varying attitudes to the status of music as property: while many do not know or do not care, some simply want cheap and easy access to music, while others are consciously critical of the quasi-monopolistic status of the corporate copyright holders and their huge profits.[3] While file sharing is sometimes presented as theft from artists, more significantly it bypasses the music distributors who would normally hold the copyright. This does not mean that their profits are thereby diminished, of course (though that seems to be their fear). As we saw in Chapter 3, illegal dissemination may also result in free exposure and a form of automatically generated advertising for musical products leading to enhanced profits (Ku 2005, 1253–4). In response to the P2P phenomenon, successive US court decisions imposed liability on those facilitating file-sharing (in particular Napster and Grokster), eventually extending secondary liability for copyright infringement to those who do little more than make it possible and intentionally 'induce' it.[4] Rather than pursue the primary infringers – the millions of people actually copying the files – it is seen to be more cost-effective and less commercially risky to pursue those who mediate the copying. (This would be a bit like suing the manufacturers of photocopiers for copyright infringements, except for the important difference that in this case the legal use of the technology is rather obvious and the manufacturers do not promote their technology as a means of getting, for instance, cheap books.) On the one hand, the end result of these legal interventions is a strengthening of copyright at the expense of technological innovation (Choi 2005–2006; Lessig 2002). On the other hand, technology is more than capable of adapting, and although the current disaggregated alternatives to Napster and Grokster may be comparably cumbersome, there is no doubt that illegal copying will continue. 'These technologies are fighting a guerrilla movement against copyright owners that will cause the courts to back off long before such technologies are meaningfully crippled' (Choi 2005–2006: 410).

Technology can therefore seemingly generate forms of resistance to private property which are demand-driven: put simply, there is an enormous demand for free music, as well as commercial benefits for those who can satisfy this demand in a way which is either legal or impractical to prosecute. In contrast, other strategies opposing private property are designed to counteract demand itself: the international campaign run as the 'Buy Nothing Day', for instance, asks people to 'participate by not participating' and to buy nothing for an entire day (Boivie 2003).[5] Buy Nothing Day is a grass-roots movement designed to counteract consumerism, and to raise consciousness of the effect of over-consumption on some key spheres of social interaction: the environment, concepts and experiences of community, and global wealth distributions.[6] Such anti-consumption campaigns might not have any direct consequences for the strictly legal concept of property, but they do challenge some of the broader cultural meanings of property including the notion that we need consumer items in order to define ourselves and our relationships (see further Chapters 2 and 4). Anti-consumption campaigns may have some small economic impact, but more importantly work on the level of ideology in an effort to alter people's consciousness about the centrality and significance of consumption. Just as property consists of cultural, historical, and theoretical layers, the rejection of property also operates in various dimensions.

REFLEXIVE APPROACHES

Opposition rarely exists for its own sake, and in fact the negative tactics mentioned above often shade into a more reflexive approach to challenging property. By 'reflexive', I mean that the rhetoric or power of property can be turned against proprietary and/or large corporate interests. This is a more self-conscious strategy than mere opposition, one which does not necessarily go as far as proposing alternative or utopian concepts of property or socio-economic relations, but which tries to draw attention to the hegemonic and ideological dimensions of excessively privatised, corporatised, or globalised property regimes.

Several examples of reflexive strategies have already been considered earlier in this book: for instance, the Lockean-inspired notion of the possessive individual has, at times, provided a rhetorical counterclaim to ideologies which commodify people. Feminists have successfully used the notion that women own their bodies to counteract broad cultural commodifications of women, and also, more specifically, to challenge legal controls on reproduction, abortion, and sexuality. Whether or not self-ownership is, in the end, a defensible notion, there is no doubt that it can be politically and tactically useful in certain contexts. Reflexive strategies can take any number of different forms and may operate at the level of positive law, broader cultural concepts of property, and its extreme expressions in the form of consumer culture.

For instance, on its face, the 'Buy Nothing' message promotes a mainly negative strategy towards property accumulation and consumerism. It simply asks consumers, for one day a year, to stop consuming, to 'spend a day without spending'.[7] This deceptively simple campaign is co-ordinated by groups such as the Adbusters Media Foundation, a Canadian-based network whose aim is to counteract the dominant culture of consumerism. They and other associated individuals and groups do not only operate negatively, however, but within a more complex and widespread set of strategies known as 'culture jamming' (see generally Lütticken 2002: 96–100; Klein 2002: 228–309; Lasn 1999). Put simply, culture jamming uses the methods of mainstream advertising to create alternative messages, for instance, via the creation of 'spoof' advertisements, such as the one which shows a number of processed foods owned by a cigarette company, the one which shows the outline of a popular vodka bottle in the shape of a noose,[8] or the one featuring half a baby's face, the caption 'she's got your eyes', and a TV set implanted where the eye should be (Lasn 1999: 5). Culture jamming can also refer to the more established and low-tech practice of defacing billboards with alternative messages. These strategies, also known as 'uncommercials', 'subvertisements' or 'anti-ads' (Lasn 1999: 128), operate by revealing the political consequences, the larger ethical questions, the hidden agendas and the assumptions embedded in mainstream advertising:

> A good jam . . . is an X-ray of the subconscious of a campaign, uncovering not an opposite meaning but the deeper truth hiding beneath the layers of advertising euphemisms.
>
> (Klein 2002: 282)

As a result, cultural capital can be reversed, making the 'cool' into the 'uncool' (Lasn 1999: 128).

Instead of mobilising more traditional activist strategies (protests, letter-writing, law reform etc.), culture jamming takes the postmodern form of fighting images with images (Lasn 1999: 123–7). It is a deliberately ironic and iterative critical cultural praxis: turning the 'same' image into something different (Carducci 2006: 122). After all, if the cultural 'text' produces subjects and ideas, rather than the other way about, then it needs to be counteracted on its own terms. An optimistic reading is that culture jamming can be seen as the dissident critical speech of *consumers*, as opposed to the more traditional free political speech of *citizens*. However, as several commentators have pointed out, culture jamming may find it hard to resist its own commodification (Klein 2002: 296–7; Lütticken 2002: 97; Carducci 2006: 124): playing the advertising game so successfully blurs the lines between object and ironic iteration and produces appealing products for those who consume anti-consumption (for instance, by wearing one of the numerous t-shirts). And as both the medium and the message are so attractive to such anti-consumption consumers, it is hardly surprising that a culture-jamming style has been reappropriated by marketers, resulting in yet more inventive efforts by culture jammers to disrupt the advertising message (Klein 2002: 297–309; Rumbo 2002: 143). Such dynamics lead some commentators to describe culture jamming as a 'war of position' in the sense described by Gramsci: 'subtle forms of contestation that are strategically aimed at transforming common sense and consciousness' (Worth and Kuhling 2004: 35; see also Rumbo 2002; cf. Gramsci

1971: 229; 238–9).[9] If culture jamming is the source of a new commercialised cool, then perhaps the purely negative tactic of buying nothing is, after all, an equally subversive (though less sophisticated and less glamorous) strategy.

To return from the problematic spheres of culture wars to a more prosaic type of law-based activism, reflexive strategies can also be seen in some appropriations of the tools and rhetoric of property in ways that alter it. A good example of such activism is to be found in the work of the Free Software Foundation (who also sell t-shirts) and the Creative Commons. The latter, for instance, is an organisation founded by several USA legal academics, who have argued in their scholarly work that intellectual property law has moved too far towards restricting and propertising the use of intangible resources at the expense of free use and the innovation that results from a vibrant public domain (Lessig 2002). The point is not to abandon copyright, but to ensure that it co-exists with a viable public domain (Lessig 2002: xvi). The Creative Commons promotes several types of copyright licences, which are less restrictive than the statutory default form of copyright:

> We use private rights to create public goods: creative works set free for certain uses. Like the free software and open-source movements, our ends are cooperative and community-minded, but our means are voluntary and libertarian.[10]

Similarly, the Free Software Foundation has devised 'copyleft' licences for software, allowing open source or free software to be released in the public domain without the risk that it will then be appropriated (as a *res nullius*) and turned into a proprietary form. Thus, it is possible freely to change and redistribute software under a copyleft licence, but only on condition that its 'free' nature is preserved.[11] The intention of Creative Commons and copyleft licences is to use existing copyright law in such a way as to counteract extensive privatisation and highly exclusive forms of intellectual property. These licences constitute a use of existing law in order to release otherwise restricted resources into the public domain. In contrast, more oppositional (and less legalistic) anti-copyright notices are sometimes found on activist publications: such opt-out notices make less effort than Creative Commons licences to 'balance' private rights with public access – indeed extensive public access of the (usually) political message is generally the entire point.

The construction of alternative forms of copyright licences is a pragmatic response to threats to the public domain. In other cases, private property threatens not so much the public domain or the public at large, but rather more limited communities and their informational and cultural resources. As I have explained in previous chapters, colonised, Indigenous and majority-world cultures have often been regarded as a target for property acquisition. In addition to the tangible items which might be significant for community or cultural identity (such as artworks, artefacts, and human remains), the frontier for acquisition of culture, broadly defined, is also intangible: traditional knowledge, art, and genetic characteristics have been expropriated and commercialised by neo-colonial commercial interests, for instance in the form of plant and DNA patents (Amani and Coombe 2005), artistic works which mimic the styles of Indigenous art (T. Davies 1996; Coleman 2005), or other cultural 'products' such as yoga (Fish 2006; for a helpful list of examples see Ziff and Rao 1997: 1–2). While some protection is offered by existing Western law (for instance copyright provides protection to individual artists), it is very limited: Western law has few means of recognising property in communally created artistic styles, rituals, or folklore (Bowrey 2001).

Although cultural 'borrowings' and the interchange of ideas is a commonplace of human co-existence, modern market-based forms of cultural appropriation often move beyond mere cultural sharing and co-operation to a more exploitative relationship, and have therefore been critiqued on a number of grounds. The ability of particular groups to determine their own identity may be removed by certain forms of cultural appropriation, especially when aesthetic styles are used by outsiders (Tsosie 2002). The distributional injustices of biopiracy, bioprospecting, and cultural appropriation have also been contested: not only is there a 'taking' in some form, but also the expropriators benefit from a kind of unjust enrichment – reaping profits which are disproportionate to their (minimal) inventive effort and capitalising on the knowledge of others (sometimes accumulated over centuries). Cultural appropriation is often underpinned by a Eurocentric failure to recognise the distinct processes of cultural production of non-Western societies (Roht-Arriaza 1997). Why is something properly known only when it has been invented and reduced to a patentable format? Moreover, there can be environmental consequences: some have pointed out that plant-based patents, such as those which applied to the Indian neem tree and basmati-related products,[12] have negative ecological consequences because their net effect is to reduce biodiversity and impose exclusive informational 'monocultures' (Shiva 1997: 69–72). The inappropriate application of patent law to so-called 'inventions' – where there is little innovation by the entity applying for the patent, no inventive step (because the 'discovery' process is routine), and where the object is a component of human life – has also been strongly challenged (Ghosh 2003: 101–2).[13]

One strategy for contesting cultural appropriation, related to the theme of this chapter, is the use of the law, discourse or language of property to characterise that which is being exploited. From the perspective of multi-national 'innovators', majority-world and Indigenous resources might be regarded simply as *res nullius*, since they have not been reduced to a form of property recognisable by Western law. This argument becomes much less compelling if the resources are themselves seen as a form of cultural property, already 'owned' by a community or cultural group, meaning that any exploitation becomes cultural theft and morally, and possibly legally, wrong. The term 'cultural property' is very well established insofar as it refers to tangible items of social value – built heritage, monuments, artefacts, the finds of archaeological digs, physical paintings, and so forth. In the past two or three decades, it has also been increasingly used to refer to intangible facets of culture: knowledge, musical and artistic styles, or rituals which define a community's identity. While the Western language of individualised and exclusive property does not map neatly (or at all) onto many of the resources, practices and relationships in question, there is little doubt that using some notion of property provides a powerful rhetorical challenge to private proprietorial interests in language recognisable to a Western audience.

To a certain degree, debate has been over how (and whether) to expand the categories of intellectual property, enabling both protection of traditional knowledge from rampant markets, as well as community-controlled commodification of certain resources (see generally Ghosh 2003; cf. Coombe 2001). However, we do not have to go very far into this topic to realise that it is fraught with controversy and competing interests, and that simply expanding the categories of 'property' without questioning its fundamental nature or concept has severe limitations. For a start, the effort to identify owners, a prerequisite to recognising some form of property, can lead to a demarcation of 'traditions' and 'culture' as static and fixed in time, place and personnel (Coleman 2005; Fitzpatrick and Joyce 2007).

Culture is denied its inherent dynamism in this process, because in order for there to be owners and objects of ownership, boundaries need to be fixed as to who owns and what they own. Problematic notions of cultural authenticity are often reinscribed by the attempt to delimit a people and their culture (Coombe 1993). Moreover, conflicting interests of ownership by all of humanity (together with the self-designated Eurocentric 'protectors' of this heritage) as against specific cultures also raises problematic questions about control of and accessibility to resources (Merryman 1986). Does 'culture' presuppose some threshold of difference and if so, from what (Ziff and Rao 1997: 3)? Commentators have also noted the incommensurability of Western notions of property with many Indigenous modes of understanding the relationship of persons to things: 'ownership' and 'property' hardly come close to expressing this relationship (Bryan 2000). And finally, therefore, 'recognising' Indigenous rights on the terms of Western law is very faint recognition and is merely a form of recolonisation by global law.

None of this is to say that the concept of cultural property should necessarily be rejected altogether – it has too great a strategic significance in counteracting dominant modes of property ownership: rather, what 'property' *is*, its own ontological characteristics, must be regarded as contestable and dynamic rather than fixed to a specific form. And importantly, extending a Western category should not be seen as any substitute for proper dialogue and negotiation with non-Western communities (see generally Roht-Arriaza 1997).

ALTERNATIVE CONCEPTIONS OF PROPERTY

The debate over cultural property underlines the limitations of the concept of property and, hence, the limitations of reflexive strategies: to some degree, property can counteract property, but in the end, alternative conceptions also need to be evoked. A pluralism of different forms of 'property' is unavoidable. Nicholas Blomley uses the term 'oppositional property narratives' to refer to evocations of property and place which contest dominant neo-liberal and privatised views of property (Blomley 2004: 97). These alternative strategies do not simply opt out of property or strategically exploit it on its own terms, but endeavour to construct different visions of the relationships between persons, things, and places. He considers the case of anti-gentrification activists in Vancouver, who constructed inclusive and relational interpretations of their local places as a way of counteracting the individualised and exclusive notion of property promoted by market-oriented development:

> Property turns out to be a site for moral conflict and struggle. For activists, however, this struggle is not simply predicated on a condemnation of the negative ethics of property but a defense of property's potential and promise. This requires, of course, a reworking of what actually counts as property, such that the collective claim of local residents may also be acknowledged as 'property'.
>
> (Blomley 2004: 103)

There may be little point in simply rejecting dominant conceptions of property: there is more opportunity to reappropriate and redefine what property means. As I have indicated above, some of the debate on cultural property has started to undertake this work; by regarding property as that which potentially brings a community together, rather than that which separates it into exclusive units. At the same time there are dangers in simply creating new and alternative forms of property if these take on an institutional form which is effectively inferior to the dominant legal forms of property: one of the (many) criticisms of native title law in Australia has been that rather than challenging the system of land ownership generally, it simply formal-ises an inferior type of title for Indigenous people – one which is inalienable and subject to extinguishment for instance (Watson 2002; Detmold 1993; Hepburn 2005). In establishing a native title claim, moreover, standards of cultural stability are demanded which would never be applied to the majority Australian cultures. While over time the concept and legal form of native title may contribute to an altered understanding of land ownership more generally (for instance through the notion of co-existing rather than exclusive uses), this is, at present, a work in progress rather than a reality.

A familiar Western example of an alternative construction of property is to be found in contemporary ideas about heritage (which is the more usual way of referring to Western cultural property). In its most recognisable form, heritage refers to the preservation of historic landmarks, monuments, or significant buildings which are recognised as having a value beyond their status as property (whether owned by government, corporations, or by private individuals). Heritage is a recognition and protection of common or social or even global value: the very idea exists in tension with the private notion of property because it assumes that the value of, say, a building, crosses the public/private division – both private proprietors and the public at large (or a section of it) may have legitimate interests in the heritage object.[14]

In recent times the concept of heritage has moved beyond the class-ridden 'stately homes' idea of what is 'of social value' to a much more inclusive, democratic, and potentially dynamic understanding (Petrie 2005). 'Heritage' is now understood to include intangible heritage, such as language, literature, and music and may be as much about spirit as about substance (Munjeri 2004).[15] It does not necessarily only represent the noble ideals of a community's past and its projected future, but incorporates dissonant, dark and controversial elements (Loulanski 2006: 211–12). It is ideally defined by communities in all of their diversity, rather than by committees of bureaucrats, and, in this sense, is dynamic and responsive to changing community values and aesthetic standards. Perhaps most significantly, this new understanding of heritage values the 'vernacular and everyday' in our cultural landscapes (Petrie 2005: 181), and is therefore potentially more inclusive than a heritage regime which merely preserves elite art and significant buildings. It actively produces cultural environments and localities, rather than simply preserving them. Indeed, as Munjeri notes, the very act of preservation under purely tangible heritage regimes actually stultifies social engagement with a site and alienates the community from it (2004): the incorporation of a wide variety of more inclusive practices into heritage principles brings together changing social values, ideas about places and landscapes, and cultural expressions. (Whether these ideals translate into effective policy is, of course, another matter: Petrie 2005.)

Concepts of heritage, and in particular community-based intangible heritage, provide a more or less officially sanctioned and often highly regulated alternative to materialistic, capitalistic, and individualised notions of market value and private property. Such concepts may subtly alter ideas about private property (and, in particular, our ideas of what property in the built environment means) and in time strengthen more abstract ideas about the communal interest in private resources. These 'communal' interests are of course not only cultural, but also environmental: the net result of heritage, planning, and environmental protection laws is that the nature of an owner's property is not fixed but can change over the duration of their ownership, particularly when this includes land.

In fact, land and diverse understandings of land, land use, and landscapes, are a core source of alternative views of property. As we saw in Chapter 3, the enclosures and clearances in England, Wales and Scotland in the Middle Ages through to Victorian times strengthened an individualistic and exclusive notion of land ownership. The enclosures were resisted, but with little long-term success. Nonetheless, the issue of land access – both rural and urban – continues to generate dissent about private ownership, both on social justice grounds, and increasingly on environmental and ecological grounds (Howkins 2002). As Howkins suggests, the importance of land to radical social justice campaigns throughout British history stands in defiance of the economic orthodoxy which sees land as of decreasing significance – at least since the industrial revolution (ibid: 2002), and even more so in the current age of technology and intellectual resources.

There still exist many direct and indirect challenges to the idea of exclusive individual property in land. For instance, a public 'right to roam' in the British countryside has for some time been promoted by the (fairly) moderate Ramblers' Association whose campaign was instrumental in the enactment of the Countryside and Rights of Way Act 2000.[16] This Act formalised a system of rights of way accessible to the public and, in this sense, promotes a notion of shared usage as opposed to completely private rights (see generally Hougie and Dickinson 2000: 230–3). The passage of the Act was preceded by some highly publicised conflicts, often involving private landowners obstructing or closing rights of way and asserting a total ability to exclude ramblers from their land. However, the reform which eventually allowed a 'right to roam' does not necessarily represent an unqualified or especially inclusive recognition of a communal interest in land. Some commentators argue that the Act is a 'careful introduction of a qualified right' which involved trade-offs by ramblers, government and landowners (Parker and Ravenscroft 2001: 394). Most interestingly, it created an 'alliance of landowners and ramblers' which had 'the ability to construct other users as deviant' (ibid: 392). 'In essence', according to Parker and Ravenscroft, 'the coalition of landowner and rambler is expedient and necessary to remake a (new) hegemony' (ibid: 392). According to this less than optimistic view, control and use of land is subject to a political compromise under which an exclusionary hierarchy of acceptable use is maintained. (Of course, there may be very good reasons for excluding certain uses or a more open access, but these are not questions

which I can go into here.) Of course, any dilution of participative/
inclusive ideals under such a reform is unsurprising: critical legal
theorists have for some time been acutely aware of the distorting
effect of trying to enshrine counter-hegemonic principles through
legislative processes. (A further example of which is the inordinately
bureaucratised process for evaluating claims under the Australian
Native Title Act 1993.)

The British land rights campaign 'The Land Is Ours' provides a
more radical example of a broad-based activist movement aimed at
reconnecting land with communities. The concept of 'land rights'
has a quite different resonance in the British context than in formerly
colonised nations, but names nonetheless the alienation of people
from land through excessive privatisation and capitalisation. It works
for objectives such as the right to roam, access to secure and afford-
able housing, and access to land-based resources.[17] The campaign
consciously associates itself with the egalitarian and communal (but
not the religious) ideals of the seventeenth-century Diggers as represented by the writings of Gerrard Winstanley. The Diggers were
politically significant in the turmoil of the English civil war for creating a political ideology of common ownership of land: this was
based on a popular interpretation of the Bible to the effect that God
gave the earth to *all* people (and not just the capitalist and colonialist
classes championed by Locke) and (pre-empting Proudhon) that private land ownership was theft from the people (Howkins 2002: 4).
The Diggers also achieved a high degree of notoriety for actually
establishing communities in several areas, and for resisting local
authorities by digging and planting the soil. Similarly, 'The Land Is
Ours' takes both an ideological (sometimes libertarian) and a practical approach to land reform, supporting a broad range of activist
interventions, mostly centred on housing and land access inequities.

Somewhere between private and common ownership of land is the
notion of stewardship, which has been described by William Lucy
and Catherine Mitchell as follows:

> The hallmark of stewardship is land holding subject to respon-
> sibilities of careful use, rather than the extensive rights to exclude,
> control and alienate that are characteristic of private property.
> The steward is, in essence, a duty-bearer, rather than a right-
> holder, but this should not be taken to suggest that the steward
> has no rights.
>
> (Lucy and Mitchell 1996: 584)

Or, as Karp puts it:

> We owe a duty of responsibility to ourselves, to our community,
> to the members of other communities on the planet, and to the
> generations to follow.
>
> (Karp 1993: 752)

The concept of stewardship has a long religious heritage,[18] but in
recent decades has been most strongly associated with environmental
protection. Proponents of stewardship have pointed out that the
choice in land control need not simply be between private and com-
mon/public ownership (Freyfogle 2006). Both ends of this spectrum
can lead to tragedies of overuse and degradation (Karp 1993: 736–7).
Stewardship of land is an appealing concept and an increasingly
popular one because it recognises the significance of land to social
justice and/or to environmental preservation and therefore to the
well-being of future world communities.[19]

Whether stewardship is a true alternative to the concept of private
property (Lucy and Mitchell 1996) or reflects an evolution or development of property (Caldwell 1986; cf. Singer 2000: 208–9) depends
largely on what 'property' is. Does it necessarily consist of 'the most
extensive rights of exclusion, control, and alienation' (Lucy and
Mitchell 1996: 586) or is it a more dynamic concept which can carry
obligations as well as rights? My own sense (no more than a guess
perhaps) is that no concept is fixed to a particular meaning and that
it is perfectly feasible to think of ownership as a concept in transition, consisting of both rights and duties. The language and consciousness of stewardship may in time contribute to an altered
understanding of what land ownership means legally and ethically.
Indeed, the extensive use of the language of stewardship in certain
areas of government policy and in the corporate sector may indicate
that this shift is already occurring.

UTOPIA AND EXPERIMENTALISM

Once again, thinking about alternatives – either in opposition to
property or as a reconstruction of it – leads us into further questions
about the entire socio-political and economic structures of society.
Some of the issues I have considered under the rubric of 'alternative
conceptions' raise a more fundamental question: is it possible to

envisage a society, including political and economic arrangements, with a more just conception of property? Exactly what 'just' consists of in this context is open to far-reaching debate. Would 'justice' be served by removing many of the state-based restrictions on private ownership, as libertarians and anarcho-capitalists argue? On the other hand, if you believe (as I do) that the institution of private property is strongly implicated in unequal distributions of power, resources, and human dignity, how can social relationships be organised (and around what kind of 'ownership') which are intrinsically less exploitative, less colonialist, less individualistic, more inclusive and more cognisant of responsibilities owed to the broader global community?

I am not about to answer these questions here, but simply wish to end the book by pointing to the existence of what might be broadly termed utopian theories and practices relating to the use of resources. The term 'utopia' deserves a little explanation. On a narrow technical definition, it does not exist, since the term 'utopia' is an invention from two Greek words meaning 'no place'.[20] Utopia is an exercise of the imagination, and can be regarded solely in that light: in that sense, to criticise a perspective as 'utopian' (that is, unrealistic or idealistic) could be seen as missing the point because utopia is hypothetical, and is deliberately constructed as such either to reveal the inadequacies of the current situation or to imagine how things might be different. On the other hand, utopian thought is arguably more expansive and more oriented to material conditions in the real world than this narrow definition suggests. Utopian thought also takes the form of positing a future society as a realistic possibility, and often contains some articulated political method for transitioning to this new society. In this sense utopia is a real place, albeit in the future. Even if the word is only a few centuries old, utopianism as a theoretical method is as old as political philosophy: one famous early example is Plato's imaginary *Republic*, which envisages the political, educational and social requirements of a just community.

Utopianisms which are based upon a perception of the injustices inherent within capitalism and private property have often taken a socialist or communist direction, and envisage the abolition or radical reconfiguration of private property in favour of state-owned or collectively owned property. Most famously, in the *Manifesto of the Communist Party*, Marx and Engels argued for the socialisation of property:

... modern bourgeois private property is the final and most complete expression of the system of producing and appropriating products that is based on class antagonisms, on the exploitation of the many by the few.

In this sense, the theory of the communists may be summed up in a single sentence: Abolition of private property.

(Marx and Engels 1965: 51)

The private property abolished under communism is not personal private property but rather the means of production which, under capitalism, is concentrated in the hands of an owning class. According to Marx and Engels, this concentration of ownership in a single class allows exploitation to occur. Since the means of production are in this way associated with social power and status, they ought to be owned by society as a whole (that is, by the state or by collectives of workers). The 'utopian' status of Marxist thought is arguable since, rather than envisaging a detailed blueprint for a new society, it concentrates on the historical progression of class struggle towards a broadly defined communist society. Nonetheless, Marxism and other forms of socialism and communism have been a significant influence on utopian thought and practice.

Anarchism is another political theory originating in the nineteenth century which directly influenced the utopianism of social dissidents throughout the twentieth century. Anarchism is a broad term meaning 'without a leader', and refers to a number of quite different and often antagonistic political philosophies. All of these are, however, sceptical of the need for institutionalised political power in the form of a state. Anarchist thought is premised on the belief that the state is counterproductive to human flourishing: the state induces apathy, avoidance of responsibility, and over-reliance on others; it represses individual expression; it creates more violence than it solves; it is corrupt; and (for some) it is economically inefficient.

Anarchism encompasses both pro- and anti-private property perspectives. Individual anarchists, anarcho-capitalists, and some right-libertarians, for instance, oppose the state because of the restrictions it places on private property, individual liberties, and the free market. Anarcho-capitalists tend to accept some version of the Lockean principles of self-ownership and appropriation through labour. The economist Murray Rothbard, for instance, argued from a Lockean basis that all rights are essentially property rights, and that the state is an illegitimate and oligarchic 'group of plunderers' or 'band of robbers' which exists on the 'parasitic exploitation' of individual property (see e.g. Rothbard 1973: 50–52). Taxation is the primary form of this state-based aggression against private property. According to Rothbard, the first principle of libertarianism is an agreement not to act aggressively against the property (including the person) of others. From that basis, and allowing the development of a capitalist market free from state interference, anarcho-capitalists argue that other 'state' functions – security, crime prevention, education, dispute resolution and so forth – could be taken up by private agencies. In contrast to Robert Nozick, who argued from similar liberal premises for a 'minimal' state, the anarchist objective is the elimination of the state altogether (Nozick 1974; cf. Rothbard 1977).

In contrast to this extreme liberalism and libertarianism, most anarchists adopt a more collectively oriented perspective which resists not only domination by the state but also the domination which flows from capitalism and unequal distributions of private property. 'Social' anarchist thought developed alongside Marxism and other forms of socialism in the nineteenth century as a class-based response to economic exploitation and inequality. However, for much of the history of these two movements, anarchists and socialists have been in conflict over the method of achieving a more just society (Hoffman 1970: 7). Much socialist thought and practice is consistent with the maintenance of the state and its associated apparatus, at least until such time as the need for state institutions has waned. Where Marxism demanded that the proletariat be raised 'to the position of the ruling class, to win the battle of democracy' (Marx and Engels 1965), anarchists such as Mikhail Bakunin argued that the state 'connotes domination and domination connotes exploitation' (Bakunin 1953: 286). Inevitably therefore a 'People's State' 'is a ridiculous contradiction, a fiction, a falsehood . . . and for the proletariat a very dangerous pitfall' (ibid). Classical anarchism rejects the state altogether (and immediately) as a form of illegitimate, violent and unnecessary hierarchy (Kropotkin 1970; Malatesta 1974). Anarchists have tended to promote 'direct action', that is, action which is unmediated by institutions such as the state: this style of political intervention is underpinned by a belief that social change is the responsibility of all people, and cannot be determined positively by a political elite or vanguard (Gordon 2007: 39–40). Thus the utopian goal of many twentieth-century anarchists was the establishment of a social order which did not rely on the power of either the state or private property as a source of law and organisation. In this way, anarchism is based on a belief in the capacity of people to organise themselves horizontally according to principles of co-operation, common ownership, mutual aid, and consensus. (Ironically, violent means of achieving this transition were regarded as necessary by some early militant anarchists, but the anarchism of recent decades has overwhelmingly tended to promote non-violent action.)

Labour movements from the nineteenth century until the present day have had an association with anarchist thought: this association was at its strongest in the late nineteenth and early twentieth centuries when anarchists were a highly visible constituent within workers' organisations (see generally Franks 2005: 230–33; Epstein 2001: 3–5). In the latter half of the twentieth century 'anarchism' (if it is possible to speak of it in the singular) changed considerably: it became more diverse in that it was no longer concerned solely with the state and class struggle but also with other forms of domination such as racism, militarism, colonialism, neo-liberal globalisation, patriarchy, and heteronormativity (Gordon 2007; Franks 2005); it has become even less organised and more like a decentralised network of movements and individuals (ibid 2007); many self-identified anarchists no longer draw inspiration directly from the political philosophy of anarchism but rather from a broad and some-times conflicting range of popular narratives generally antithetical to hierarchy and property (Epstein 2001); and finally, anarchism no longer appears to offer a realistic *immediate* option for organising the entire population of a country. One key focus of contemporary anarchism is neo-liberal globalisation (Epstein 2001; Gordon 2007), though this does not necessarily translate into resistance to *all* forms of private property and capitalism. The concept of 'parecon' or participatory economics is another expression of contemporary anti-capitalist globalisation or alternative globalisation thought. Parecon is anarchist in ethos (if not in explicit orientation) since it promotes the idea of the co-operative participation of all people in economic planning, for instance through worker ownership and management of production.[21]

The realisation that a broad-scale social revolution is not imminent has not motivated anarchist activists and thinkers to abandon their critique of the state, but rather to concentrate upon direct action and a 'prefigurative' style of politics. As Uri Gordon puts it, this '[translates] into a commitment to "being the change", on any level from personal relationships that address sexism and racism to sustainable living and communes' (Gordon 2007: 40). 'Being the change' might involve decision-making by consensus, organising through decentralised collectives rather than top-down hierarchies, accepting a level of dynamism and instability in group processes, and creating new methods of distributing resources within communal settings.[22] Such practices are often experimental and 'post-utopian', rather than expressly utopian: they 'prefigure' the future by trying to enact the principles of a better society in the here and now. The concept of prefigurative politics is based on the claim that a better society will not be attained by wholesale change or revolution led by the few. It must be created incrementally from the bottom up: this is the only way to promote broad change in social values and perceptions. Or, to quote Gordon again, '[c]ollectively-run grassroots projects are, on this account, the seeds of a future society "within the shell of the old" ' (ibid).

Many attempts have been made to put utopian, experimental, and prefigurative ideas into some form of practice. World history is full of examples of the creation of small 'intentional communities' which represent a retreat from current conditions and an attempt to reform society. (World history is also full of examples of entirely new states created intentionally following a revolution, but I do not focus on them here.) The tradition of deliberately creating a community to live out the good or just life is as strong now as it has ever been. Intentional communities reinvent society around distinct values, which can be artistic, religious or spiritual, egalitarian, land-sharing, environmental, libertarian, or some blend of these (Metcalf 1995).[23] In many cases an ethos of social justice, co-operation, anti-authoritarianism and a critique of the values and practices associated with private property are also present. For instance, I have already mentioned the mid-seventeenth century Diggers who, motivated both by need and by ideals of common ownership of land (Howkins 2002: 3–4), attempted to establish agricultural communities in rural England. In Australia in the 1890s, a large number of 'utopian experiments' resulted in socialist communities which were in effect a practical and ideological response to drought and economic recession (Metcalf 1995: 18–30). Most famously, throughout the twentieth century and up to the present time, the kibbutzim of Israel have been based on broad socialist principles such as mutual aid and joint ownership of property. Contemporary intentional communities also include eco-villages, eco-farms, housing co-operatives, and other forms of land and house-sharing, as well as religious communities.

Although many intentional communities do occupy a particular geographical site or space separated (by varying degrees) from mainstream society, more broadly there are also virtual spaces and other intentional practices which form non-geographically bounded communities. Virtual communities interact through technical media – chat rooms, wikis, and blogs, for instance – and some of this online communal activity constitutes a form of resistance to the hegemony of private property. I have already mentioned, for instance, some web-based communities such as the open source software movement, which creates and promotes 'free' software. The common practice of 'sharing' music and video files, in itself a form of resistance to property (albeit often an illegal one), is also supported by online communities. On the ground, there are also food co-operatives and trading schemes whose members opt out of mainstream consumerism by forming their own economic units and complementary currencies. Such a system may simply be a practical response to the needs of a local community or, like many anarchist organisations, may self-consciously prefigure an alternative to capitalist property-practices.

CONCLUSION

There is hardly a satisfactory conclusion to be drawn from all of this – this chapter, and indeed this entire book. As usual, I will not pretend to conclude, so perhaps it is best to end the book the same way I started, with a cliché:

> The first person who, having fenced off a plot of ground, took it into his head to say *this is mine* and found people simple enough to believe him, was the true founder of civil society. What crimes, wars, murders, what miseries and horrors would the human race have been spared by someone who, uprooting the stakes or filling in the ditch, had shouted to his fellow-men: Beware of listening to this impostor; you are lost if you forget that the fruits belong to all and the earth to no-one! But it is very likely that by then things had already come to the point where they could no longer remain as they were. For this idea of property, depending on many prior ideas which could only have arisen successively, was not conceived all at once in the human mind. It was necessary to make much progress, to acquire much industry and

enlightenment, and to transmit and augment them from age to age, before arriving at this last stage of the state of nature.

(Rousseau 1978: 31)

Rousseau's state of nature as described here is not a singular state at all but an infinite regress of ideas and therefore hardly 'natural': the foundation of civil society in the taking of private property turns out not to be a single critical event but rather a generations-long progression towards that end (cf. Derrida 1978: 292). Despite the dubious status of 'nature' and the arbitrariness of the founding point of civil society, however, Rousseau was right about the complex production of the idea of property, a point which I hope to have conveyed in various ways throughout this book. Moreover, despite many fine efforts at conceptualising utopia, the future of property or resource management is also not going to be 'conceived all at once in the human mind' but will rather be lived, contested, and prefigured in multiple contexts and according to diverse values.

Notes

1 In the *Grokster* case, it was reported that 'billions of files are shared across peer-to-peer networks each month': *MGM Studios Inc v Grokster* 545 US 913.
2 See e.g. Blomley 2004: 20, on squatting, as well as the UK-based Advisory Service for Squatters at www.squatter.org.uk (viewed 29 March 2007).
3 Artists, moreover, are sometimes critical of the ways in which copyright law stifles creativity, especially when their work consciously involves sampling and modifying existing works. See e.g. the Negativland website: www.negativland.com.
4 For a good introduction to the case see Hall 2006, and for a more extensive analysis see Shih Ray Ku 2005.
5 www.buynothingday.co.uk; see also www.adbusters.org.
6 Ibid.
7 BND 2006 Media Release http://adbusters.org/metas/eco/bnd/view.php?id=315, viewed 23 March 2007.
8 http://adbusters.org/spoofads/index.php.
9 For more thorough discussions of culture jamming, especially with reference to its artistic predecessors, 'Situationism', and its role in establishing a counter-hegemony, see Worth and Kuhling 2004 and Lütticken 2002.
10 http://creativecommons.org/about/history, viewed 26 March, 2007.
11 See 'What is Copyleft?' at http://www.gnu.org/copyleft/. Free does not refer to price, but to the ability to use, copy, change and redistribute the software: http://www.gnu.org/gnu/gnu-history.html.

12 Neem, which has a wide variety of medicinal and agricultural uses, was the basis of several products which were patented by a US company in the 1980s. Vandana Shiva reports that after this company set up operations in India, the price of neem rose 'beyond the reach of the ordinary people' and that '[p]oor people have lost access to a resource vital for their survival – a resource that was once widely and cheaply available to them' (Shiva 2001: 59).

13 None of this should be taken to suggest that the Indigenous community has not shown ingenuity and innovation in construction of art, medicine, and knowledge – all too often traditional forms of knowledge are seen as a part of the *natural* development of the community (and thus, like all natural things, up for grabs), rather than a distinct cultural product.

14 Of course, heritage – such as cultural property – can itself be commercialised and made into an economic object: Loulanski 2006: 209.

15 I will not cite all of the national and international instruments relating to this issue, but for a recent statement see the UNESCO Convention for the Safeguarding of Intangible Cultural Heritage 2003, Article 2, available at http://www.unesco.org/culture/ich/index.php?pg=00006 (viewed 4 October 2007).

16 www.ramblers.org.uk (viewed 29 March 2007).

17 See generally www.tlio.org.uk (viewed 29 March 2007).

18 See for instance the Interfaith Council for Environmental Stewardship 'Cornwall Declaration' available at http://www.stewards.net/ CornwallDeclaration.htm (viewed 2 April 2007).

19 Feeling virtuous, on Tuesday this week (the last of March 2007) I caught the bus home from work and, thinking I might do it more than once, bought a ticket valid for multiple trips. The ticket came inside a little folder on which was printed the (now clichéd) words 'We don't inherit the Earth from our parents . . . but borrow it from our children'. The optimist in me would like to think that this indicates how common and popular the language of stewardship has become, but the sceptic in me sees it as just another marketing campaign for public transport. (The pluralist in me thinks both perspectives are true.)

20 See the Oxford English Dictionary, which provides the etymology of utopia as 'οὐ not + τόπ-ος a place'. The word was apparently first coined by Sir Thomas More in his book *Utopia*.

21 See generally the resources published on Znet at http://www.zmag.org/ parecon/indexnew.htm.

22 Some of these practices, for instance consensus decision-making, were adopted from other social movements of the twentieth century, in particular feminism.

23 See also the transcript of the Radio National (Australia) programme 'Re-imagining Utopia' at www.abc.net.au/rn/utopias/programs/life_ matters.htm, viewed 19 April 2007.

References

Althusser, L. (1994), 'Ideology and Ideological State Apparatuses', in S. Žižek (ed.), *Mapping Ideology*, London: Verso.

Amani, B. and Coombe, R. (2005), 'The Human Genome Diversity Project: The Politics of Patents at the Intersection of Race, Religion, and Research Ethics', *Law and Policy*, 27(1): 152–88.

Aoki, K. (1996), '(Intellectual) Property and Sovereignty: Notes Toward a Cultural Geography of Authorship', *Stanford Law Review*, 48: 1293–355.

Archard, D. (1993), 'Do Parents Own their Children?', *International Journal of Children's Rights*, 1: 293–301.

Aristotle (1962), *The Politics*, Middlesex: Penguin.

Armitage, D. (2004), 'John Locke, Carolina, and the Two Treatises of Government', *Political Theory*, 32: 602–27.

Arneil, B. (1994), 'Trade, Plantations, and Property: John Locke and the Economic Defense of Colonialism', *Journal of the History of Ideas*, 55: 591–609.

Arneil, B. (1996), *John Locke and America: The Defence of English Colonialism*, Oxford: Clarendon Press.

Arneil, B. (2001), 'Women as Wives, Servants and Slaves: Rethinking the Public/Private Divide', *Canadian Journal of Political Science/Revue canadienne de science politique*, 34, 29–54.

Atiyah, P. (1979), *The Rise and Fall of Freedom of Contract*, Oxford: Clarendon Press.

Austin, J. (1954), 'The Province of Jurisprudence Determined' in H.L.A. Hart (ed.) *The Province of Jurisprudence Determined and The Uses of the Study of Jurisprudence*, London: Weidenfeld and Nicolson.

Avery, C., Jolls, C., Posner, R. and Roth, A. (2001), 'The Market for Federal Judicial Law Clerks', *University of Chicago Law Review*, 68: 793–901.

Baker, J.H. (1990), *An Introduction to English Legal History*, 3rd edn, London: Butterworths.

Bakunin, M. (1953), *The Political Philosophy of Bakunin* (compiled and edited by G.P. Maximoff) Illinois: Free Press.

Bannister, J. (2006), *Secret Business and Business Secrets: The Hindmarsh Island Bridge Affair, Information Law and the Public Sphere*, Australian National University: Unpublished doctoral dissertation.

Barrad, C.V.M. (1993), 'Genetic Information and Property Theory', *Northwestern University Law Review*, 87: 1037–86.

Becker, L. (1980), 'The Moral Basis of Property Rights' in J. Pennock and J. Chapman (eds) *Property*, New York: New York University Press.

Bell, D. (1995), 'Property Rights in Whiteness – Their Legal Legacy, Their Economic Costs', in R. Delgado (ed.), *Critical Race Theory*, Philadelphia: Temple University Press.

Bell, S., Henry, J. and Wray, R. (2004), 'A Chartalist Critique of John Locke's Theory of Property, Accumulation, and Money: or, is it Moral to Trade Your Nuts for Gold', *Review of Social Economy*, 62: 51–65.

Benkler, Y. (1999), 'Free as the Air to Common Use: First Amendment Constraints on Enclosure of the Public Domain', *New York University Law Review*, 74: 354–446.

Bennington, G. (1993), 'Derridabase', in G. Bennington and J. Derrida, *Jacques Derrida*, trans. G. Bennington, Chicago: University of Chicago Press.

Bentham, J. (1931), *Theory of Legislation*, London: Kegan Paul.

Bentham, J. (1970), *An Introduction to the Principles of Morals and Legislation*, J.H. Burns and H.L.A. Hart (eds), London: The Athlone Press.

Berkes, F., Feeny, D., McKay, B.J. and Acheson, J.M. (1989), 'The Benefits of the Commons', *Nature*, 340 (13 July): 91–3.

Bernasconi, R. (2001), 'Who Invented the Concept of Race?' in R. Bernasconi (ed) *Race*, Oxford: Blackwell Publishers.

Berns, S. (1993) 'Women in English Legal History: Subject (almost), Object (irrevocably), Person (not quite)', *University of Tasmania Law Review*, 12: 26–56.

Blackstone, L.R. (2005), 'A New Kind of English: Cultural Variance, Citizenship and DiY Politics amongst the Exodus Collective in England', *Social Forces*, 84: 803–20.

Blackstone, W. (1765), *Commentaries on the Laws of England, Volume I, Of the Rights of Persons*, Oxford: Clarendon Press.

Blackstone, W. (1766), *Commentaries on the Laws of England, Volume II, Of the Rights of Things*, Oxford: Clarendon Press.

Blomley, N. (2004), *Unsettling the City: Urban Land and the Politics of Property*, New York: Routledge.

Boivie, I. (2003), 'Buy Nothing, Improve Everything', *The Humanist*, 63 (6): 7–9.

Bottomley, A. (2007), 'A Trip to the Mall: Revisiting the Public/Private Divide' in H. Lim and A. Bottomley (eds), *Feminist Perspectives on Land Law*, Abingdon: Routledge-Cavendish.

Bowrey, K. (2001), 'The Outer Limits of Copyright Law – Where Law Meets Philosophy and Culture', *Law and Critique*, 12: 75–98.

Boyle, J. (1992), 'A Theory of Law and Information: Copyright, Spleens, Blackmail, and Insider Trading', *California Law Review*, 80: 1413–540.

Boyle, J. (2003), 'The Second Enclosure Movement and the Construction of the Public Domain', *Law and Contemporary Problems*, 66: 33–74.

Brace, L. (2001), 'Husbanding the Earth and Hedging out the Poor', in A.R. Buck, J. McLaren, and N. Wright (eds), *Land and Freedom: Law, Property rights and the British Diaspora*, Aldershot: Ashgate-Dartmouth.

Brooks, R. (2003), 'Ancient Slavery Versus American Slavery: A Distinction with a Difference', *University of Memphis Law Review*, 33: 265–75.

Brown, W. (2003), 'Gender in Counterpoint', *Feminist Theory*, 4: 365–8.

Bryan, B. (2000), 'Property as Ontology: on Aboriginal and English Understandings of Property', *Canadian Journal of Law and Jurisprudence*, 13: 3–31.

Buck, A.R. (2001), ' "Strangers in their own land": Capitalism, Dispossession, and the Law' in A.R. Buck, J. McLaren, and N. Wright (eds), *Land and Freedom: Law, Property Rights and the British Diaspora*, Aldershot: Ashgate-Dartmouth.

Bush, J. (1993), ' "You're Gonna Miss Me When I'm Gone": Early Modern Common Law Discourse and the Case of the Jews', *Wisconsin Law Review*, 1993: 1225–85.

Butler, J. (1993), *Bodies That Matter: On the Discursive Limits of 'Sex'*, New York: Routledge.

Butler, J. (1994), 'Against Proper Objects', *Differences: A Journal of Feminist Cultural Studies*, 6: 1–26.

Cahir, J. (2004), 'The Withering Away of Property: The Rise of the Internet Information Commons', *Oxford Journal of Legal Studies*, 24: 619–41.

Calabresi, G. (1991), 'Do We Own Our Bodies?', *Health Matrix*, 1: 5–18.

Caldwell, L.K. (1986), 'Land and the Law: Problems in Legal Philosophy', *University of Illinois Law Review*, 1986: 319–35.

Carducci, V. (2006), 'Culture Jamming: A Sociological Perspective', *Journal of Consumer Culture*, 6(1): 116–38.

Carlson, D.G. (2000), 'How to Do Things with Hegel', *Texas Law Review*, 78: 1377–97.

Carrington, S. (2003), 'Capitalism and Slavery and Caribbean Historiography: An Evaluation', *Journal of African American History*, 88: 304–12.

Castles, A. (1982), *An Australian Legal History*, Sydney: Law Book Company.

Chambers, R. (2001), *An Introduction to Property Law in Australia*, Sydney: L.B.C. Information Services.

Choi, B. (2005–2006), 'The Grokster Dead-End', *Harvard Journal of Law and Technology*, 19: 393–411.

Christman, J. (1986), 'Can Ownership be Justified by Natural Rights?', *Philosophy and Public Affairs*, 15: 156–77.

Chryssostalis, J. and Tuitt, P. (2005), 'Introduction', *Law and Critique*, 16: 1.

Cohen, F. (1935), 'Transcendental Nonsense and the Functional Approach', *Columbia Law Review*, 35: 809–49.

Cohen, F. (1954), 'Dialogue on Private Property', *Rutgers Law Review*, 9: 357–87.

Cohen, M. (1927), 'Property and Sovereignty', *Cornell Law Quarterly*, 13: 8–30.

Coleman, E.B. (2005), *Aboriginal Art, Identity and Appropriation*, Aldershot: Ashgate.

Conaghan, J. (1998), 'Tort Litigation in the Context of Intra-Familial Abuse', *Modern Law Review*, 61: 132–61.

Coombe, R. (1993), 'The Properties of Culture and the Politics of Possessing Identity: Native Claims in the Cultural Appropriation Controversy', *Canadian Journal of Law and Jurisprudence*, 6: 249–85.

Coombe, R. (2001), 'The Recognition of Indigenous Peoples' and Community Traditional Knowledge in International Law', *St Thomas Law Review*, 14: 275–85.

Cooper, D. (2004), *Challenging Diversity: Rethinking Equality and the Value of Difference*, Cambridge: Cambridge University Press.

Cooper, D. (2007), 'Opening Up Ownership: Community Belonging, Belongings, and the Productive Life of Property', *Law and Social Inquiry*, 32: 625–66.

Cotterrell, R. (1987), 'Power, Property and the Law of Trusts: A Partial Agenda for Critical Legal Scholarship', in P. Fitzpatrick and A. Hunt (eds), *Critical Legal Studies*, Oxford: Blackwell.

Crabtree, L. (2006), 'Disintegrated Houses: Exploring Ecofeminist Housing and Urban Design Options', *Antipode*, 38: 711–34.

Dallmayr, F. (1991), 'Rethinking the Hegelian State', in D. Cornell, M. Rosenfeld and D. G. Carlson (eds), *Hegel and Legal Theory*, New York: Routledge.

Dangelo, K. (1989), 'How Much of You Do You Really Own? A Property Right in Identity', *Cleveland State Law Review*, 37: 499–524.

Daunton, M.J. (1995), 'Open Fields and Enclosure: The Demise of Commonality', in M.J. Daunton, *Progress and Poverty: An Economic and Social History of Britain 1700–1850*, Oxford: Oxford University Press.

Davies, M. (1994), 'Feminist Appropriations: Law, Property and Personality', *Social and Legal Studies*, 3: 365–91.

Davies, M. (1996), *Delimiting the Law: 'Postmodernism' and the Politics of Law*, London: Pluto Press.

Davies, M. (1998), 'The Proper: Discourses of Purity', *Law and Critique* 9: 147–73.

Davies, M. (1999), 'Queer Persons, Queer Property: Self-Ownership and Beyond', *Social and Legal Studies*, 8: 327–52.

Davies, M. (2002a), 'Ethics and Methodology in Legal Theory: A (Personal) Research Anti-Manifesto', *Law Text Culture*, 6: 7–26.

Davies, M. (2002b), *Asking the Law Question: The Dissolution of Legal Theory*, Sydney: Lawbook Co.

Davies, M. and Naffine, N. (2001), *Are Persons Property? Legal Debates About Property and Personality*, London: Ashgate.

Davies, T. (1996), 'Aboriginal Cultural Property?', *Law in Context*, 14(2): 1–28.

Derrida, J. (1974), *Of Grammatology*; trans. Gayatri Chakravorty Spivak, Baltimore: Johns Hopkins University Press.

Derrida, J. (1977), 'Limited Inc. a b c . . .', *Glyph*, 2: 162–254.

Derrida, J. (1978), *Writing and Difference*, London: Routledge and Kegan Paul.

Derrida, J. (1985), 'Des Tours de Babel', in J. Graham (ed.), *Difference in Translation*, Ithaca: Cornell University Press.

Derrida, J. (1988), *The Ear of the Other*, Lincoln: University of Nebraska Press.

Derrida, J. (1991), 'Force of Law: The "Mystical Foundation of Authority" ', *Cardozo Law Review*, 11: 919–1045.

Detmold, M. (1993), 'Law and Difference: Reflections on Mabo's Case', *Sydney Law Review*, 15: 159–67.

Diósdi, G. (1970), *Ownership in Ancient and Preclassical Rome*, Budapest: Académiai Kiadó.

Dorsett, S. (1995), 'Civilization and Cultivation: Colonial Policy and Indigenous peoples in Canada and Australia', *Griffith Law Review*, 4: 214–38.

Dorsett, S. and McVeigh, S. (2002), 'Just So: "The Law Which Governs Australia is Australian Law" ', *Law and Critique*, 13: 289–309.

Douzinas, C. (2005), 'Oubliez Critique', *Law and Critique*. 16: 47–69.

Douzinas, C. and Geary, A. (2005), *Critical Jurisprudence: The Political Philosophy of Justice*, Oxford: Hart Publishing.

Douzinas, C., Warrington, R. and McVeigh, S. (1991), *Postmodern Jurisprudence: The Law of Text in the Texts of Law*, London: Routledge.

Drahos, P. (1996), *A Philosophy of Intellectual Property*, Aldershot: Dartmouth.

Drahos, P. and Braithwaite, J. (2002), *Information Feudalism: Who Owns the Knowledge Economy?*, London: Earthscan Publications.

Edejer, T.T. (1999), 'North–South Research Partnerships: the Ethics of

Carrying our Research in Developing Countries', *British Medical Journal*, 319: 438–41.

Eden, S. (2005), 'Green, Gold and Grey Geography: Legitimating Academic and Policy Expertise', *Transactions of the Institute of British Geographers*, 30: 282–86.

Edgeworth, B. (1988), 'Post-Property: A Postmodern Conception of Private Property', *University of New South Wales Law Journal*, 11: 87–116.

Eleftheriadis, P. (1996), 'The Analysis of Property Rights', *Oxford Journal of Legal Studies*, 16: 31–53.

Engels, F. (1968), 'Socialism: Utopian and Scientific', in K. Marx and F. Engels, *Selected Works*, London: Lawrence and Wishart.

English, P. (2007), 'Ancient Monuments of National Importance: Symbols of Whose Past?' in H. Lim and A. Bottomley (eds), *Feminist Perspectives on Land Law*, Abingdon: Routledge-Cavendish.

Epstein, B. (2001), 'Anarchism and the Anti-Globalization Movement', *Monthly Review*, 53: 1–14.

Ertman, M. and Williams, J. (eds) (2005), *Rethinking Commodification*, New York: New York University Press.

Ewing, K. (1990), 'The Illusion of Wholeness: Culture, Self, and the Experience of Inconsistency', *Ethos*, 18: 251–78.

Filmer, R. (1949), *Patriarcha and Other Political Works of Sir Robert Filmer*, P. Laslett (ed.), Oxford: Basil Blackwell.

Fish, A. (2006), 'The Commodification and Exchange of Knowledge in the Case of Transnational Commercial Yoga', *International Journal of Cultural Property*, 13: 189–206.

Fitzpatrick, P. and Joyce, R. (2007), 'Copying Right: Cultural Property and the Limits of (Occidental) Law', in Fiona Macmillan (ed.), *New Directions in Copyright Law*, London: Edward Elgar Publishing.

Flanagan, T. (1989), 'The Agricultural Argument and Original Appropriation: Indian Lands and Political Philosophy', *Canadian Journal of Political Science/Revue canadienne de science politique*, 22: 589–602.

Foucault, M. (1972), *The Archaeology of Knowledge*, London: Tavistock.

Foucault, M. (1979), 'What Is an Author?', in J. Harari, *Textual Strategies: Perspectives in Post-Structuralist Criticism*, Ithaca: Cornell University Press.

Foucault, M. (1980), *Power/Knowledge: Selected Interviews and Other Writings 1972–1977*, Brighton: Harvester Press.

Franks, B. (2005), 'British Anarchism and the Miners' Strikes', *Capital and Class*, 87: 227–54.

Freeman, M.D.A. (1983), *The Rights and Wrongs of Children*, London: Frances Pinter.

Freyfogle, E. (2006), 'Goodbye to the Public–Private Divide', *Environmental Law Journal*, 36: 7–24.

Frow, J. (1995), 'Elvis' Fame: The Commodity Form and the Form of the Person', *Cardozo Studies in Law and Literature*, 7: 131–71.

Gaus, G. (1994), 'Property, Rights, and Freedom', *Social Philosophy and Policy*, 11: 209–40.

Geertz, C. (1979), 'From the Native's Point of View: On the Nature of Anthropological understanding', in P. Rabinow and W.M. Sullivan (eds), *Interpretive Social Science: A Reader*, Berkeley: University of California Press.

Ghosh, S. (2003), 'Globalization, Patents, and Traditional Knowledge', *Columbia Journal of Asian Law*, 17: 73–120.

Gieryn, T. (1999), *Cultural Boundaries of Science: Credibility on the Line*, Chicago: University of Chicago Press.

Godden, L. (2003), 'Grounding Law as Cultural Memory: A "Proper" Account of Property and Native Title in Australian Law and Land', *Australian Feminist Law Journal*, 19: 61–80.

Goodrich, P. (1983), 'The Antinomies of Legal Theory: An Introductory Survey', *Legal Studies*, 3: 1–20.

Gordon, U. (2007), 'Anarchism Reloaded', *Journal of Political Ideologies*, 12: 29–48.

Gramsci, A. (1971), *Selections from the Prison Notebooks*, New York: International Publishers.

Gray, K. (1991), 'Property in Thin Air', *Cambridge Law Journal*, 50: 252–307.

Gray, K.J. and Symes, P.D. (1981), *Real Property and Real People: Principles of Land Law*, London: Butterworths.

Gray, K. and Gray, S.F. (1999), 'Private Property and Public Propriety', in J. McLean (ed.), *Property and the Constitution*, Oxford: Hart.

Grey, T. (1980), 'The Disintegration of Property', *Nomos*, 22: 69–85.

Gunnarsson, Å., Burman M. and Wennberg L. (2004), 'Economic Dependence and Self-Support in Family, Tax and Social Law', in E. Svensson, A. Pylkkänen and J. Niemi-Kiesiläinen (eds), *Nordic Equality at a Crossroads: Feminist Legal Studies Coping with Difference*, Aldershot: Ashgate.

Hall, H. (2006), 'The Day the Music Died: The Supreme Court's Reversal of *MGM Studios Inc v Grokster* and its Impact on Secondary Liability for Copyright Infringement', *Journal of Law and Education*, 35: 387–93.

Hann, C.M. (ed.) (1998), *Property Relations: Renewing the Anthropological Tradition*, Cambridge: Cambridge University Press.

Hardin, G. (1968), 'The Tragedy of the Commons', *Science*, 162: 1243–48.

Harris, C. (1993), 'Whiteness as Property', *Harvard Law Review*, 106: 1707–91.

Harris, J.W. (1996), 'Who owns My Body', *Oxford Journal of Legal Studies*, 16: 55–84.

Hart, H.L.A. (1994), *The Concept of Law*, 2nd edn, Oxford: Clarendon Press.

Hart, S. (1991), 'From Property to Person Status: Historical Perspective on Children's Rights', *American Psychologist*, 46: 53–9.

Hasday, J.E. (2000), 'Contest and Consent: A Legal History of Marital Rape', *California Law Review*, 88: 1373–505.

Heald, P. (2003–2004), 'The Rhetoric of Biopiracy', *Cardozo Journal of International and Comparative Law*, 11: 519–46.

Hegel, G.W.F. (1952, first published 1821), *Philosophy of Right*, trans. T.M. Knox, Oxford: Oxford University Press.

Hegel, G.W.F. (1975), *Hegel's Logic (Being Part one of the Encyclopaedia of the Philosophical Sciences (1830))*, trans. W. Wallace, Oxford: Clarendon Press.

Heller, M. (1999), 'The Boundaries of Private Property', *Yale Law Journal*, 108: 1163–223.

Hepburn, S. (2005), 'Feudal Tenure and Native Title: Revising an Enduring Fiction', *Sydney Law Review*, 27: 49–86.

Hoffman, R. (1970), 'Introduction', in R. Hoffman (ed.), *Anarchism*, New York: Atherton Press.

Hohfeld, W.N. (1913), 'Fundamental Legal Conceptions as Applied in Judicial Reasoning', *Yale Law Journal*, 23: 16.

Hohfeld, W.N. (1917), 'Fundamental Legal Conceptions as Applied in Judicial Reasoning', *Yale Law Journal*, 26: 710–70.

Honoré, A.M. (1961), 'Ownership', in A.G. Guest (ed.), *Oxford Essays in Jurisprudence*, London: Oxford University Press.

Horkheimer, M. (1972), 'Traditional and Critical Theory', in M. Horkheimer, *Critical Theory: Selected Essays*, New York: Continuum.

Hougie, D.J.P. and Dickinson, J. (2000), 'The Right to Roam – What's In a Name? Policy Development and Terminology Issues in England and Wales, UK', *European Environment*, 10: 230–38.

Howkins, A. (2002), 'From Diggers to Dongas: the Land in English Radicalism 1649–2000', *History Workshop Journal*, 54: 1–23.

Hsueh, V. (2006), 'Cultivating and Challenging the Common: Lockean Property, Indigenous Traditionalisms, and the Problem of Exclusion', *Contemporary Political Theory*, 5: 193–214.

Irigaray, L. (1985), *This Sex Which is Not One*, Ithaca: Cornell University Press.

Jaensch, D. (2002), *Community Access to the Parliamentary Electoral Processes in South Australia since 1850: A Research Report*, Rose Park, SA: State Electoral Office.

Jameson, F. (1994), 'Postmodernism and the Market', in S. Žižek (ed.) *Mapping Ideology*, London: Verso.

Janke, T. (1998), *Our Culture, Our Future: Report on Australian Indigenous Cultural and Intellectual Property Rights*, Canberra: AIATSIS.

Johnston, D. (1999), *Roman Law in Context*, Cambridge: Cambridge University Press.

Kant, I. (1929), *Critique of Pure Reason*, London: Macmillan.

Kant, I. (1930), *Lectures on Ethics*, trans. L. Infield, London: Methuen.

Kant, I. (1952), *Critique of Judgement*, Oxford: Clarendon Press.

Kant, I. (1988), 'Foundations of the Metaphysics of Morals', in L. W. Beck (ed.), *Kant: Selection*, New York: Macmillan.

Karp, J. (1993), 'A Private Property Duty of Stewardship: Changing our Land Ethic', *Environmental Law*, 23: 735–62.

Kelsen, H. (1991), *General Theory of Norms*, trans. M. Hartney, Oxford: Clarendon Press.

Kelsen, H. (1992), *Introduction to the Problems of Legal Theory, A Translation of the First Edition of the Reine Rechtslehre or Pure Theory of Law 1934*, trans. B. Litschewski Paulson and S. Paulson, Oxford: Clarendon Press.

Kelsey, J. (1995), 'Restructuring the Nation: The Decline of the Colonial Nation-State and Competing Nationalisms in Aotearoa/New Zealand', in P. Fitzpatrick (ed.), *Nationalism, Racism and the Rule of Law*, Aldershot: Dartmouth Publishing.

Klein, N. (2002), *No Logo: No Space, No Choice, No Jobs*, New York: Picador.

Kropotkin, P. (1970), *Kropotkin's Revolutionary Pamphlets*, New York: Dover Publications.

Ku, R.S.R. (2005), 'Grokking Grokster', *Wisconsin Law Review*, 2005: 1217–82.

Laclau, E. (1996), *Emancipation(s)*, London: Verso.

Landes, E. and Posner, R. (1978), 'The Economics of the Baby Shortage', *Journal of Legal Studies*, 7: 323–48.

Lange, D. (1981), 'Recognizing the Public Domain', *Law and Contemporary Problems*, 44: 147–78.

Lasn, K. (1999), *Culture Jam: The Uncooling of America™*, New York: Eagle Brook.

Lattas, J. (1989), 'Feminism as a Proper Name', *Australian Feminist Studies*, 9: 85–96.

Lebovics, H. (1986), 'The Uses of America in Locke's Second Treatise of Government', *Journal of the History of Ideas*, 47: 567–81.

Lessig, L. (2002), *The Future of Ideas*, New York: Vintage Books.

Levi-Strauss, C. (1969), *Elementary Structures of Kinship,* London: Eyre and Spottiswoode.

Locke, J. (1988), *Two Treatises on Government* (first published in 1690), P. Laslett (ed.), Cambridge: Cambridge University Press.

Loulanski, T. (2006), 'Revising the Concept of Cultural Heritage: The Argument for a Functional Approach', *International Journal of Cultural Property*, 13: 207–33.

Lucy, W. and Mitchell, C. (1996), 'Replacing Private Property: The Case for Stewardship', *Cambridge Law Journal*, 55: 566–600.

Lukács, G. (1971), *History and Class Consciousness*, London: Merlin Press.

Lütticken, S. (2002), 'The Art of Theft', *New Left Review*, 13: 89–104.

Lyotard, J-F. (1984), *The Postmodern Condition: A Report on Knowledge*, trans. G. Bennington and B. Massumi, Minneapolis: University of Minnesota Press.

MacKinnon, C. (1982), 'Feminism, Marxism, Method and the State: An Agenda for Theory', *Signs*, 7: 515–44.

MacPherson, C.B. (1964), *The Political Theory of Possessive Individualism: Hobbes to Locke*, Oxford: Clarendon Press.

Maine, H. (1920; 10th edn), *Ancient Law: Its Connection with the Early History of Society, and its Relation to Modern Ideas*, London: John Murray.

Maitland, F.W. (1897), *Domesday Book and Beyond: Three Essays in the Early History of England*, Cambridge: Cambridge University Press; Boston: Little, Brown and Co.

Malatesta, E. (1974), *Anarchy*, London: Freedom Press.

Marx, K. (1845), 'Theses on Feuerbach', in K. Marx and F. Engels (1968), *Selected Works*, London: Lawrence and Wishart.

Marx, K. (1859), 'Preface to *The Critique of Political Economy*', in K. Marx and F. Engels (1968), *Selected Works*, London: Lawrence and Wishart.

Marx, K. (1947), *Capital: A Critical Analysis of Capitalist Production* (originally published 1887), Volume I, edited by F. Engels, trans. S. Moore and E. Aveling New York: International Publishers.

Marx, K. and Engels, F. (1965), *Manifesto of the Communist Party*, Beijing: Foreign Languages Press.

Mayes, C. (1957), 'The Sale of Peerages in Early Stuart England', *Journal of Modern History*, 29: 21–37.

McCoin, S. (1998), 'Law and Sex Status: Implementing the Concept of Sexual Property', *Women's Rights Law Reporter*, 19: 237–45.

McKean, M. (1992), 'Success on the Commons: A Comparative Examination of Institutions for Common Property Resource Management', *Journal of Theoretical Politics*, 4: 247–81.

McLean, I., Spirling, A. and Russell, M. (2003), 'None of the Above: The UK House of Commons Votes on Reforming the House of Lords, February 2003', *Political Quarterly*, 74: 298–310.

McLean, J. (ed.) (1999a), *Property and the Constitution*, Oxford: Hart Publishing.

McLean, J. (1999b), 'Property as Power and Resistance', in J. McLean (ed.), *Property and the Constitution*, Oxford: Hart Publishing.

Melissaris, E. (2004), 'The More the Merrier? A New Take on Legal Pluralism', *Social and Legal Studies*, 13: 57–79.

Merry, S.E. (1988), 'Legal Pluralism', *Law and Society Review*, 22: 869–96.

Merryman, J.H. (1986), 'Two Ways of Thinking About Cultural Property', *American Journal of International Law*, 80: 831–53.

Metcalf, B. (1995), *From Utopian Dreaming to Communal Reality: Co-operative Lifestyles in Australia*, Sydney: University of New South Wales Press.

Mgbeoji, I. (2006), *Global Biopiracy: Patents, Plants, and Indigenous Knowledge*, Vancouver: UBC Press.

Moran, L. and Skeggs, B. (2001), 'The Property of Safety', *Journal of Social Welfare and Family Law*, 23: 379–93.

Moreton-Robinson, A. (2005a), 'The Possessive Logic of Patriarchal White Sovereignty: The High Court and the Yorta Yorta Decision', *borderlands e-journal* 3.

Moreton-Robinson, A. (2005b), 'The House the Jack Built: Britishness and White Possession', *Australian Critical Race and Whiteness Studies Association Journal*, 1: 21–9.

Motha, S. (2002), 'The Sovereign Event in a Nation's Law', *Law and Critique*, 13: 311–38.

Munjeri, D. (2004), 'Tangible and Intangible Heritage: from difference to convergence', *Museum International*, 56(1–2): 12–20.

Murphy, T., Roberts, S. and Flessas, T. (4th edn, 2004), *Understanding Property Law*, London: Sweet and Maxwell.

Murray, D.W. (1993), 'What is the Western Concept of the Self? On Forgetting David Hume', *Ethos*, 21: 3–23.

Naffine, N. (1997), 'The Body Bag', in N. Naffine and R. Owens (eds), *Sexing the Subject of Law*, Sydney: LBC information Services.

Naffine, N. (1998), 'The Legal Structure of Self-Ownership: Or the Self-Possessed Man and the Woman Possessed', *Journal of Law and Society*, 25: 193–212.

Nedelsky, J. (1990), 'Law, Boundaries, and the Bounded Self', *Representations*, 30: 162–89.

Nedelsky, J. (1993), 'Property in Potential Life? A Relational Approach to Choosing Legal Categories', *Canadian Journal of Law and Jurisprudence*, 6: 343–65.

Nietzsche, F.W. (1954a), 'On Truth and Lies in an Extra-Moral Sense (1873)' in W. Kaufman (ed. and trans.), *The Portable Nietzsche*, New York: Penguin.

Nietzsche, F.W. (1954b), 'Notes (1873)', in W. Kaufman (ed. and trans.), *The Portable Nietzsche*, New York: Penguin.

Nozick, R. (1974), *Anarchy, State and Utopia*, Oxford: Blackwell Publishers.

Nundy, S. and Gulhati, C. (2005), 'A New Colonialism? – Conducting Clinical Trials in India', *New England Journal of Medicine*, 352: 1633–6.

Nwabueze, R. (2002), 'Biotechnology and the New Property Regime in Human Bodies and Body Parts', *Loyola of Los Angeles International and Comparative Law Review*, 24: 19–64.

Ochoa, T. (2003), 'Origins and Meanings of the Public Domain', *University of Dayton Law Review*, 28: 215–67.

Ost, F. and Van de Kerchove, M. (2002), *De la pyramide au réseau: pour une théorie dialectique du droit*, Brussels: Publications des Facultés Universitaires Saint-Louis.

Ostrom, E. and Hess, C. (2003), 'Ideas, Artifacts, and Facilities: Information as a Common-Pool Resource', *Law and Contemporary Problems*, 66: 111–45.

Ostrom, E., Burger, J., Field, C., Norgaard, R., and Policansky, D. (1999), 'Revisiting the Commons: Local Lessons, Global Challenges', *Science*, 284 (9 April): 278–82.

Parekh, B. (1995), 'Liberalism and Colonialism: A Critique of Locke and Mill', in J. Nederveen Pieterse and B. Parekh (eds), *The Decolonization of the Imagination: Culture, Knowledge and Power*, New Jersey: Zed Books.

Parker, G. and Ravenscroft, N. (2001), 'Land, Rights, and the Gift: *The Countryside and Rights of Way Act 2000* and the Negotiation of Citizenship', *Sociologia Ruralis*, 41: 381–98.

Pateman, C. (1988), *The Sexual Contract*, Cambridge: Polity Press.

Paulson, S. (1992), 'The Neo-Kantian Dimension of Kelsen's Pure Theory of Law', *Oxford Journal of Legal Studies*, 12: 311–32.

Pavlich, G. (2005), 'Experiencing Critique', *Law and Critique*, 16: 95–112.

Penner, J.E. (1997), *The Idea of Property in Law*, Oxford: Clarendon Press.

Perkin, J. (1989), *Women and Marriage in Nineteenth Century England*, London: Routledge.

Petchesky, R. (1995), 'The Body as Property: A Feminist Re-vision', in F. Ginsburg and R. Rapp (eds), *Conceiving the New World Order: The Global Politics of Reproduction*, Berkeley: University of California Press.

Petrie, L. (2005), 'An Inherently Exclusionary Regime: Heritage Law – the South Australian Experience', *Macquarie Law Journal*, 5: 177–99.

Phillips, J. and Wetherell, C. (1995), 'The Great Reform Act of 1832 and the Political Modernization of England', *American Historical Review*, 100: 411–36.

Posner, R. (1992), *Sex and Reason*, Cambridge, Mass.: Harvard University Press.

Pottage, A. (1998), 'Instituting Property', *Oxford Journal of Legal Studies*, 18: 331–44.

Pottage, A. (2004), 'Who Owns Academic Knowledge?', *Cambridge Anthropology*, 24: 1–20.

Pottage, A. and Mundy, M. (eds) (2004), *Law, Anthropology and the Constitution of the Social: Making Persons and Things*, Cambridge: Cambridge University Press.

Proudhon, P-J. (1994), *What Is Property?*, Cambridge: University Press.

Radin, M. (1987), 'Market-Inalienability', *Harvard Law Review*, 100: 1840–937.

Radin, M. (1993), *Reinterpreting Property*, Chicago: University of Chicago Press.

Radin, M. (1996), *Contested Commodities*, Cambridge, Mass: Harvard University Press.

Raff, M. (1988), Environmental Obligations and the Western Liberal Property Concept', *Melbourne University Law Review*, 22: 657–92.

Rassam, A.Y. (1999), 'Contemporary Forms of Slavery and the Evolution of the Prohibition of Slavery and the Slave Trade Under Customary International Law', *Virginia Journal of International Law*, 39: 303–52.

Reich, C. (1964), 'The New Property', *Yale Law Journal*, 73: 733–87.

Reich, C. (1991), 'The Individual Sector', *Yale Law Journal*, 100: 1409–48.

Reynolds, H. (1987), *Frontier: Reports from the Edge of White Settlement*, St Leonards, NSW: Allen and Unwin.

Richards, E. (2000), *The Highland Clearances: People, Landlords, and Rural Turmoil*, Edinburgh: Birlinn.

Roberts, L. (1987), 'Who Owns the Human Genome', *Science*, 237: 358–61.

Roht-Arriaza, N. (1997), 'Of Seeds and Shamans: The Appropriation of the Scientific and Technical Knowledge of Indigenous and Local Communities', in B. Ziff and P. Rao (eds), *Borrowed Power: Essays on Cultural Appropriation*, New Brunswick: Rutgers University Press.

Rose, C. (1994), *Property and Persuasion: Essays on the History, Theory, and Rhetoric of Ownership*, Boulder, Colorado: Westview Press.

Rose, C. (2003), 'Romans, Roads, and Romantic Creators: Traditions of Public Property in the Information Age', *Law and Contemporary Problems*, 66: 89–110.

Rose, C. (2005), 'Whither Commodification?', in M.Ertman and J. Williams (eds), *Rethinking Commodification*, New York: New York University Press.

Rose, D.B. (1999), 'Indigenous Ecologies and an Ethic of Connection', in N. Low (ed.), *Global Ethics and Environment*, London: Routledge.

Rose, G. (1984), *Dialectic of Nihilism*, Blackwell: Oxford.

Rothbard, M. (1973), *For a New Liberty: The Libertarian Manifesto*, New York: Collier Books (online edition 2002).

Rothbard, M. (1977), 'Robert Nozick and the Immaculate Conception of the State', *Journal of Libertarian Studies*, 1: 45–57.

Rousseau, J-J. (1978), 'The Origin of Inequality', extract reprinted in C.B. MacPherson (ed.), *Property: Mainstream and Critical Positions*, Oxford: Basil Blackwell.

Rumbo, J. (2002), 'Consumer Resistance in a World of Advertising Clutter: The Case of Adbusters', *Psychology and Marketing*, 19 (2): 127–48.

Ryan, A. (1994), 'Self Ownership, Autonomy, and Property Rights', *Social Philosophy and Policy*, 11: 241–58.

Salter, M. (1987), 'Justifying Private Property Rights: A Message from Hegel's Jurisprudential Writings', *Legal Studies*, 3: 245–62.

Samuel, G. (1999), 'The Many Dimensions of Property', in J. McLean (ed.), *Property and the Constitution*, Oxford: Hart Publishing.

Saussure, F. de (1959), *Course in General Linguistics*, New York: Philosophical Library.

Schnably, S. (1993), 'Property and Pragmatism: A Critique of Radin's Theory of Property and Personhood', *Stanford Law Review*, 45: 347–407.

Schochet, G. (1989), Review: Radical Politics and Ashcraft's Treatise on Locke', *Journal of the History of Ideas*, 50: 491–510.

Schroeder, J. (1994a), 'Chix Nix Bundle-O-Stix: A Feminist Critique of the Disaggregation of Property', *Michigan Law Review*, 93: 239–319.

Schroeder, J. (1994b), 'Virgin Territory: Margaret Radin's Imagery of Personal Property as the Inviolate Feminine Body', *Minnesota Law Review*, 79: 55–171.

Schroeder, J. (1995), 'The Vestal and the Fasces: Property and the Feminine in Law', *Cardozo Law Review*, 16: 805–924.

Sherman, B. and Bently, L. (1999), *The Making of Intellectual Property Law*, Cambridge: Cambridge University Press.

Shiva, V. (1997), *Biopiracy: The Plunder of Nature and Knowledge*, Boston: South End Press.

Shiva, V. (2001), *Protect or Plunder: Understanding Intellectual Property Right*, London: Zed Books.

Silverman, K. (1983), *The Subject of Semiotics*, New York: Oxford University Press.

Simon, A. (2006), 'Cows as Chairs: Questioning Categorical Legal Distinctions in a Non-Categorical World', in M. Hauser, F. Cushman and M. Kamen (eds), *People, Property, or Pets?*, Indiana: Purdue University Press.

Simpson, A.W.B. (2nd edn, 1986), *A History of the Land Law*, Oxford: Clarendon Press.

Singer, B. (1991), 'The Right of Publicity: Star Vehicle or Shooting Star?', *Cardozo Arts and Entertainment Law Journal*, 10: 1–49.

Singer, J.W. (2000), *Entitlement: The Paradoxes of Property*, New Haven: Yale University Press.

Skeggs, B. (2004), 'Exchange, Value and Affect: Bourdieu and "the Self" ', *Sociological Review*, 52 (Supplementary Issue 2): 75–95.

Smith, S. (1992), 'Hegel and the Problem of Slavery', *Cardozo Law Review*, 13: 1771–815.

Sökefeld, M. (1999), 'Debating Self, Identity, and Culture in Anthropology', *Current Anthropology*, 40: 417–31.

Spiro, M. (1993), 'Is the Western Conception of the Self "Peculiar" within the Context of the World Cultures?', *Ethos*, 21: 107–53.

Stewart, I. (1998), 'Kelsen Tomorrow', *Current Legal Problems*, 51: 181–204.

Stone, L. (1958), 'The Inflation of Honours 1558–1641', *Past and Present*, 14: 45–70.

Stretton, T. (1998), *Women Waging Law in Elizabethan England*, Cambridge: Cambridge University Press.

Svensson, E. (2007), 'Boundary Work in Legal Scholarship', in A. Gunnarsson, E. Svensson, and M. Davies (eds), *Exploiting the Limits of Law: Swedish Feminism and the Challenge to Feminism*, Aldershot: Ashgate.

Svensson, E. and Pylkkänen, A. (2004), 'Contemporary Challenges in Nordic Feminist Legal Studies', in E. Svensson, A. Pylkkänen and J. Niemi-Kiesiläinen (eds), *Nordic Equality at a Crossroads: Feminist Legal Studies Coping with Difference*, Aldershot: Ashgate.

Tate, W.E. (1967), *The English Village Community and the Enclosure Movements*, London: Gollancz.

Taylor, C. (1975), *Fields in the English Landscape*, London: JM Dent and Sons.

Thomas, J.A.C. (1975), *The Institutes of Justinian: Text, Translation, and Commentary*, Amsterdam: North Holland Publishing Company.

Thomas, J.A.C. (1976), *Textbook of Roman Law*, Amsterdam: New Holland Publishing.

Thomas, P. (2003), 'Property's Properties: From Hegel to Locke', *Representations*, 84: 30–43.

Thomas, S.M., Davies, A.R.W., Birtwistle, N.J., Crowther, S.M., and Burke, F.J. (1996), 'Ownership of the Human Genome', *Nature*, 380 (4 April): 387–8.

Thompson, E.P. (1968), *The Making of the English Working Class*, Harmondsworth: Penguin.

Tsosie, R. (2002), 'Reclaiming Native Stories: An Essay on Cultural Appropriation and Cultural Rights', *Arizona State Law Journal*, 34: 299–358.

Tully, J. (1993), *An Approach to Political Philosophy: Locke in Contexts*, Cambridge: Cambridge University Press.

Turner, M. (1984), *Enclosures in Britain 1750–1830*, London: Macmillan.

Underkuffler, L. (1990), 'On Property: An Essay', *Yale Law Journal*, 100: 127–48.

Vandevelde, K. (1980), 'The New Property of the Nineteenth Century: The Development of the Modern Concept of Property', *Buffalo Law Review*, 29: 325–67.

Vinogradoff, P. (1957), 'Feudalism', *Cambridge Medieval History* 3, 458–84.

Wacquant, L. (2004), 'Critical Thought as Solvent of Doxa', *Constellations*, 11: 97–101.

Waldron, J. (1988), *The Right to Private Property*, Oxford: Clarendon.

Warner, K. (2000), 'Sentencing in Cases of Marital Rape: Towards Changing the Male Imagination', *Legal Studies*, 20: 592–611.

Watkin, T.G. (1999), *An Historical Introduction to Modern Civil Law*, Aldershot: Ashgate.

Watson, I. (1997), 'Indigenous Peoples' Law-Ways: Survival Against the Colonial State', *Australian Feminist Law Journal*, 8: 39–58.

Watson, I. (2002), 'Buried Alive', *Law and Critique*, 13: 253.

Weaver, J. (2005), 'Concepts of Economic Improvement and the Social Construction of Property Rights: Highlights from the English-Speaking World', in J. McLaren, A.R. Buck and N. Wright (eds), *Despotic Dominion: Property Rights in British Settler Societies*, Vancouver: UBC Press.

Williams, M. (1970), 'The enclosure and reclamation of waste land in England and Wales in the eighteenth and nineteenth centuries', *Transactions of the Institute of British Geographers*, 51: 55–69.

Williams, P. (1987), 'Alchemical Notes: Reconstructing Ideals from Deconstructed Rights', *Harvard Civil Rights – Civil Liberties Law Review*, 22: 401–33.

Wise, S. (1999), 'Animal Thing to Animal Person – Thoughts on Time, Place, and Theories', *Animal Law*, 5: 61–8.

Wittgenstein, L. (1958), *Philosophical Investigations*, trans. G.E.M. Anscombe, Oxford: Basil Blackwell.

Wittig, M. (1992), 'On the Social Contract', in *The Straight Mind and Other Essays*, London: Harvester Wheatsheaf.

Woodmansee, M. (1984), 'The Genius and the Copyright: Economic and Legal Conditions of the Emergence of the "Author" ', *Eighteenth Century Studies*, 17: 425–48.

Worth, O. and Kuhling, C. (2004), 'Counter-hegemony, anti-globalisation and culture in International Political Economy, *Capital and Class*, 84: 31–42.

Ziff, B. and Rao, P. (1997), 'Introduction to Cultural Appropriation: A Framework for Analysis', in B. Ziff and P. Rao (eds), *Borrowed Power: Essays on Cultural Appropriation*, New Jersey: Rutgers University Press.

Žižek, S. (1994), 'The Spectre of Ideology', in S. Žižek (ed.), *Mapping Ideology*, London: Verso.

Zucker, R. (1993), 'Unequal Property and Subjective Personality in Liberal Theories', *Ratio Juris*, 6: 86.

Index